First World War
and Army of Occupation
War Diary
France, Belgium and Germany

40 DIVISION
119 Infantry Brigade,
Brigade Machine Gun Company
16 June 1916 - 28 February 1918

WO95/2607/4

The Naval & Military Press Ltd
www.nmarchive.com
Published in association with The National Archives

Published by

The Naval & Military Press Ltd

Unit 10 Ridgewood Industrial Park,

Uckfield, East Sussex,

TN22 5QE England

Tel: +44 (0) 1825 749494

www.naval-military-press.com

www.nmarchive.com

This diary has been reprinted in facsimile from the original. Any imperfections are inevitably reproduced and the quality may fall short of modern type and cartographic standards.

© **Crown Copyright**
Images reproduced by permission of The National Archives, London, England, 2015.

Contents

Document type	Place/Title	Date From	Date To
Heading	WO95/2607/4		
Heading	119th Machine Gun Coy. Jun 1916-Feb 1918		
War Diary	Grantham	16/06/1916	16/06/1916
War Diary	Southampton	16/06/1916	16/06/1916
War Diary	Le Havre	17/06/1916	18/06/1916
War Diary	Bruay	19/06/1916	03/07/1916
War Diary	Les Brebis	04/07/1916	31/10/1916
Heading	War Diary 119th M.G. Coy Nov from 1st 1916 to Nov 30th 1916		
War Diary	Bruay	01/11/1916	01/11/1916
War Diary	Orlencourt	02/11/1916	02/11/1916
War Diary	Pt. Houvin	03/11/1916	04/11/1916
War Diary	Rousefay	05/11/1916	05/11/1916
War Diary	Montigny	06/11/1916	09/11/1916
War Diary	Grimont	09/11/1916	15/11/1916
War Diary	Wavans	16/11/1916	17/11/1916
War Diary	Villers L'Hopital	18/11/1916	18/11/1916
War Diary	Neuvillette	19/11/1916	19/11/1916
War Diary	Le Souich	20/11/1916	22/11/1916
War Diary	Beauval	23/11/1916	23/11/1916
War Diary	Barlette	24/11/1916	24/11/1916
War Diary	Epagne	25/11/1916	30/11/1916
Heading	War Diary of 119th Machine Gun Coy, from Dec.1.16 to Dec.31.16.		
War Diary	Epagne	01/12/1916	10/12/1916
War Diary	Les Celestins	10/12/1916	26/12/1916
War Diary	Camp 17 Suzanne	27/12/1916	27/12/1916
War Diary	Le Foret	28/12/1916	04/01/1917
War Diary	Camp 17	05/01/1917	07/01/1917
War Diary	Bouchavesnes	08/01/1917	18/01/1917
War Diary	Camp 17	19/01/1917	22/01/1917
War Diary	Le Foret	23/01/1917	27/01/1917
War Diary	Camp 12	28/01/1917	10/02/1917
War Diary	Camp 17	11/02/1917	11/02/1917
War Diary	Rancourt	12/02/1917	22/02/1917
War Diary	Camp 111	23/02/1917	28/02/1917
Heading	119th M.G. Coy from march 1-March 31 1917 Vol 10		
War Diary	Camp 111 Grovetown	01/03/1917	08/03/1917
War Diary	Camp 19 Clery	09/03/1917	16/03/1917
War Diary	Camp 17 Suzanne	17/03/1917	19/03/1917
War Diary	Curlu	20/03/1917	20/03/1917
War Diary	Haut Allaines	21/03/1917	21/03/1917
War Diary	Aizecourt Le Haut	22/03/1917	25/03/1917
War Diary	Bouchavesnes	26/03/1917	31/03/1917
Heading	War Diary For 119th M.G. Coy. For April 1917		
War Diary	Bouchavesnes	01/04/1917	06/04/1917
War Diary	Etricourt	07/04/1917	17/04/1917
War Diary	Fins	18/04/1917	22/04/1917
War Diary	Gouzeaucourt	23/04/1917	30/04/1917
Miscellaneous	119th Infantry Brigade. Appendix A		

Type	Description	Date From	Date To
Miscellaneous	119th Machine Gun Coy.	25/04/1917	25/04/1917
Map			
Heading	War Diary of 119th M.G. Coy. from May. 1.17 to May 31.17		
War Diary	Gouzeaucourt	01/05/1917	05/05/1917
War Diary	Gouzeaucourt	06/05/1917	06/05/1917
War Diary	In The Line	07/05/1917	12/05/1917
War Diary	In The Field Gouzeaucourt	13/05/1917	22/05/1917
War Diary	Gouzeaucourt	23/05/1917	26/05/1917
War Diary	Fins	27/05/1917	31/05/1917
Miscellaneous	From O.C. 119th M.G. Coy.		
Heading	119th Machine Gun Coy War Diary For June 1917		
War Diary	Fins	01/06/1917	02/06/1917
War Diary	Villers Plouich	03/06/1917	18/06/1917
War Diary	Fins	19/06/1917	22/06/1917
War Diary	In The Field Dessart Wood	23/06/1917	26/06/1917
War Diary	Gonnelieu	26/06/1917	30/06/1917
Heading	War Diary 119th M.G. Company July 1917		
War Diary	In The Field Gonnelieu	01/07/1917	31/07/1917
Miscellaneous	Statement Of Strength Etc		
Heading	War Diary 119 M.G. Company From August 1st 1917 To Aug 31st 1917		
War Diary	Gonnelieu	01/08/1917	13/08/1917
War Diary	Heudicourt	14/08/1917	29/08/1917
War Diary	Gonnelieu	30/08/1917	31/08/1917
Map			
Miscellaneous	Operation Order 119th Machine Gun Coy Appendix III		
Miscellaneous	Operation Orders Central 119th M.G. Coy.		
Operation(al) Order(s)	Operation Order No. 3 Appendix IV.		
Miscellaneous	Training Orders of Capt of Amery Parking Appendix V		
Miscellaneous	Appendix V		
Operation(al) Order(s)	Operation Order No. 4 By Capt. D.g. Amery Parkes Commanding 119th M.G. Coy.	30/08/1917	30/08/1917
Miscellaneous			
Miscellaneous	Copy I		
Heading	War Diary 119 Machine Gun Company From September 1st 1917 To September 30th 1917		
War Diary	Gonnelieu	01/09/1917	20/09/1917
War Diary	Gouzeaucourt	20/09/1917	30/09/1917
Miscellaneous	Appendix I		
Operation(al) Order(s)	Operation Orders No. 5 by Capt. D.J. Amery-Parkes Commanding 119th M.G.C.C. Appendix II		
Miscellaneous	Appendix II		
Miscellaneous			
Operation(al) Order(s)	Operation Order No. 6 by Capt. D.J. Amery-Parkes Cmd. 119th M G Coy Appendix III	12/09/1917	12/09/1917
Miscellaneous	Appendix III		
Miscellaneous			
Operation(al) Order(s)	40th In Divisional Machine Gun Company. Operation Orders No. 21		
Map			
Miscellaneous	40th. Divisional Machine Gun Company.	19/09/1917	19/09/1917
Miscellaneous	Appendix IV		
Heading	War Diary 119 Machine Gun Company. October 1917		
War Diary	Gouzeaucourt	01/10/1917	07/10/1917
War Diary	Heudicourt	08/10/1917	08/10/1917

Type	Description	Start	End
War Diary	Peronne	09/10/1917	10/10/1917
War Diary	Monchiet	11/10/1917	29/10/1917
War Diary	Humbercourt	30/10/1917	31/10/1917
War Diary		01/10/1917	31/10/1917
Operation(al) Order(s)	Operation Order No. 7 By Capt D.J. Amery-Parkes Cmd M G Coy Appendix II	03/10/1917	03/10/1917
Miscellaneous	Order For Move 119th M.G. Coy. Oct 8th 1917. Appendix III	08/10/1917	08/10/1917
Miscellaneous	Relief Orders By Capt D.J. Amery-Parkes Cmd 119th M G Coy. Appendix IV		
Miscellaneous	Orders For Brigade Scheme Appendix V		
Heading	War Diary 119 M.G. Coy. No 1		
Miscellaneous	Personnel For Trains Etc		
Heading	War Diary 119th Machine Gun Company November 1917		
War Diary	Humbercourt	01/11/1917	16/11/1917
War Diary	Monchiet	16/11/1917	16/11/1917
War Diary	Gomiecourt	17/11/1917	18/11/1917
War Diary	Barastre	19/11/1917	20/11/1917
War Diary	Doignies	21/11/1917	25/11/1917
War Diary	Lechelle	26/11/1917	26/11/1917
War Diary	Pommier	27/11/1917	30/11/1917
Miscellaneous	Appendix I		
Miscellaneous	119th Machine Gun Company	29/11/1917	29/11/1917
Heading	War Diary 119th Machine Gun Coy. Dec 1917		
War Diary	Pommier	01/12/1917	02/12/1917
War Diary	St Leger	03/12/1917	10/12/1917
War Diary	Ervillers	11/12/1917	12/12/1917
War Diary	St Leger	05/12/1917	09/12/1917
War Diary	Ervillers	13/12/1917	13/12/1917
War Diary	Railway U.25.a.7.4	14/12/1917	24/12/1917
War Diary	St Leger	25/12/1917	31/12/1917
Miscellaneous	Appendix I		
Heading	War Diary 119th M G Company January 1918		
War Diary	Ervillers	01/01/1918	05/01/1918
War Diary	St Legers	08/01/1918	11/01/1918
War Diary	Ervillers	11/01/1918	14/01/1918
War Diary	St Leger	14/01/1918	31/01/1918
Miscellaneous	Appendix I		
Heading	War Diary 119 Machine Gun Company February 1918		
War Diary	Ervillers	01/02/1918	11/02/1918
War Diary	Neuville Vitasse	11/02/1918	27/02/1918
War Diary	Ervillers	28/02/1918	28/02/1918
Miscellaneous	Appendix I		

woods 2607/4

40TH DIVISION
119TH INFY BDE

119TH MACHINE GUN COY.
JUN 1916-FEB 1918

WAR DIARY or INTELLIGENCE SUMMARY

Army Form C. 2118.

(Erase heading not required.)

119 Bste M.G. Corps June

Place	Date	Hour	Summary of Events and Information	Remarks and references to Appendices
Grantham	16/6/16	00.10	Train left for Southampton	
Southampton	16/6/16	16.00	3 officers and 40 men left in Bellerophon for Havre. Rest of Company left in Caesarea; crossing rough, and many men ill.	
Le Havre	17/6/16	9.00	Troops from Caesarea disembarked, and marched to meet Transport disembarking from Bellerophon.	
		17.00	Finished disembarkation and marched to rest Camp; held hot mapochan; 1 mile exchange	
	18/6/16	16.00	Marched to Gare des Marchandises and entrained, leaving 21.00.	
	19/6/16	22.00	Arrived, and marched to excellent billets at La Ferme De la Buche near Auchen	
		23.00	O.C. reported personally to Div H.Q.	
Bruay	20/6/16	9.50	2/Lt Anderton + Hawkmore left by car for Bulley Grenay for instructions in the Trenches	
			Company employed all day in cleaning up billet.	
	21/6/16		a.m. Drill and training	
			p.m. Cleaning up for inspection by G.O.C. 1st Army	
	22/6/16		a.m. Cleaning up for inspection	
		15.00	Inspected by G.O.C. 1st Army; 7 generals in all present.	
			2/Lt Anderton + Hawkmore returned from Bulley Grenay.	AGM

Army Form C. 2118.

WAR DIARY
or
INTELLIGENCE SUMMARY
(Erase heading not required.)

Instructions regarding War Diaries and Intelligence Summaries are contained in F.S. Regs., Part II and the Staff Manual respectively. Title Pages will be prepared in manuscript.

Place	Date	Hour	Summary of Events and Information	Remarks and references to Appendices
Bruay	23/6/16		Ordinary training carried out.	
		10.00	O.C. proceeded to Bde H.Q. at Marles, and thence to Les Brebis, making arrangements for attachment of officers and men to 2nd M.G. Coy for instruction in trenches	
		20.00	O.C. returned. Pte Gowan reported suffering from cerebro-spinal meningitis; all arrangements cancelled and whole Coy isolated. Very bad thunderstorm 16.00	
		21.30	O.C. proceeded to Marles re spotted fever case	
	24/6/16	01.30	O.C. returned from Marles.	
		08.00	A.D.M.S. arrived and released Coy from quarantine excepting 31 men	
			O.C. proceeded to Marles, and return a.m.	
		20.00	Ordinary training carried out. Whole Coy released from isolation. First mail bag arrived, mainly consisting of demands for returns	
	25/6/16	11.00	2/Lts Birchall, Herbert, Groves and Turner with 70 O.R. proceeded to Les Brebis to report to the 2nd Bde. M.G. Coy for instruction, rationed by Coy up to 26th in lorries.	
		14.00	O.C. proceeded to Labussière to Field Cashier's office, and return.	
	26/6/16		Ordinary training carried out	
	27/6/16	7.00	O.C. Coy and 2/Lt Anderton proceeded to Les Brebis to see part of Coy training in trenches. Trenches very bad in spite of rain, and moderately quiet. O.C. Coy arrived with O.C. 2nd Bde M.G. Coy re shortage of establishment as allowed by W.O.	AFW
		19.00	O.C. Coy + 2/Lt Anderton returned	

Army Form C. 2118.

WAR DIARY
or
INTELLIGENCE SUMMARY
(Erase heading not required.)

Instructions regarding War Diaries and Intelligence Summaries are contained in F. S. Regs., Part II. and the Staff Manual respectively. Title Pages will be prepared in manuscript.

Place	Date	Hour	Summary of Events and Information	Remarks and references to Appendices
Pernes	28/6/16	9.00	O.C. proceeded to Marles-les-Mines to see Bde H.Q. re attached men.	
			Orders issued to part of Coy. in trenches at 29th ovng to continued activity to leave Marles-les-Mines.	
		16.00	G.e. returned from Marles-les-Mines.	
			Sent applicantion to HQ Bde asking for extra men and giving reasons.	
			Weather wet. Coy have made mule lines in Vau Const Kain.	
	29/6/16	6 am	One limber, 24 officers' chargers left for LES BREBIS to bring back officers and their kit.	
		19.00	Coy. returned from trenches, with exception of 3 ORs. left behind owing to order not having reached them.	
			43 men and 7 officers attached to Coy for training in M.G. work; taken accompanied their officers.	
		16.30	O.C. proceed to Bde H.Q. and return re. foundation of 142nd Bde front.	
			Training for attached men started in P.m.	
		20.00	Bdn. Coy. 10 Warter men, 30 W. Yorks sergeants, with officers during afternoon.	
			Weather fine; breezes and trenches drying up.	
	30/6/16		2nd in command paying kits.	
			Instructional class carried on.	
			Company practising trench scheme.	

A.J. Manning Capt

40 Army Form C. 2118.
July
119 M.G.C.
Vol 2

WAR DIARY
or
INTELLIGENCE SUMMARY
Army Form C. 2118.

(Erase heading not required.)

Place	Date	Hour	Summary of Events and Information	Remarks and references to Appendices
Amay	1/7/16	10.00	Ordinary training carried out. Gas lecture and demonstration given	
		15.00	Bathing parade.	
	2/7/16	8.00	O.C. 2nd Lt. Gustafson, Burchett, and Herbert proceeded to Les Brebis HQr 1st Bde M.G. Coy re taking over Colonnes sector of trenches, and returned. 1st Bde M.G. Cy emplacements tilled, mule lines and general arrangements very good.	
	3/7/16	a.m.	Company preparing to move in.	
		16.00	and joined night column 18th Bn. Welsh Regt. under Lt. Col. R. Grant Thorold at X roads I.24.d.9.9. near Division, and proceeded via Houdain and Maisnil Les Ruitz to Barlin, thence to Bois Dolhain, arriving 10 p.m. The men and mules stay tired.	
Les Brebis	4/7/16	4.30	Left Bois Dolhain and marched via Hersin and Sains to Les Brebis, arriving 8.00. Relief took place immediately, being completed at 13.00. 2/Lt Anderson and No. 1 section, and 1 gun No. 4 section on right — the left — 2/Lt. Burchett and No. 2 section, 2/Lt. Herbert and No. 3 section, + 2 guns of No. 4 section in reserve. 2 M.G. Corps men and 2 attached men sent with each gun.	
	5/7/16		Situation normal; 30 mm (well around Donkey's Post.	
	6/7/16		24 more infantry men (6 from each battalion) attached, so as to enable proper relief to be carried out. Situation normal.	

WAR DIARY or INTELLIGENCE SUMMARY

Army Form C. 2118.

Place	Date	Hour	Summary of Events and Information	Remarks and references to Appendices
LES BRÉBIS	7/7/16	12.00	Situation normal, but front line and support trenches on right badly damaged by T.M. fire. Indirect overhead fire carried out by 1 gun.	
		22.00	Indirect overhead night firing carried out throughout the night with 4 guns.	
	8/7/16	4.08	S.O.S. Signal sent out.	
		4.18	S.O.S. Signal cancelled; apparently a false alarm (no attack).	
	9/7/16	9.00	Internal relief carried out; 2/Lt. Grant relieving 2/Lt. BURCHETT, and 2/Lt. HARKNESS relieving 2/Lt. ANDERTON; Lieut. HIGHAM relieved 2/Lt. HERBERT in reserve. Indirect fire was used from Trench line on to enemy's Communications.	
	9/7/16		Indirect fire was again used.	
		22.30	Gas alarm was raised; some heavy shelling by enemy Trench mortars.	
	10/7/16		Enemy were very quiet; indirect fire was used at night.	
	11/7/16		Enemy very quiet; indirect fire was stopped, as Lieut. HIGHAM failed to adjust & correct his guns – 2/Lt. ANDERTON relieved Lieut. HIGHAM, who returned to Bry H.Q. pending further instructions: Pte VILLARS very slightly wounded.	
	12/7/16		Relief (internal) carried out; 2/Lt. TURNER and HERBERT Coy in front line.	

Army Form C. 2118.

WAR DIARY
or
INTELLIGENCE SUMMARY

(Erase heading not required.)

Instructions regarding War Diaries and Intelligence Summaries are contained in F.S. Regs., Part II. and the Staff Manual respectively. Title Pages will be prepared in manuscript.

Place	Date	Hour	Summary of Events and Information	Remarks and references to Appendices
LES BREBIS	13/7/16		Indirect fire was used during the night in CITÉ DE ROLLENCOURT. Enemy very quiet; one attached man wounded.	
	14/7/16		Enemy bombarded TEMPLE STREET, CALONNE with 5.9's. Indirect fire was used at night.	
	15/7/16		Indirect fire was again used during the night. Lewis guns fired on Corps in wire; the enemy were very quiet.	
	16/7/16	9.00	Internal relief carried out; 2/Lts BURCHETT and GROVES went into support and front line positions; 2/Lt. ANDERSON remained in reserve line.	
		13.00	2/Lt. HARKNESS proceeded to HOUCHIN to attend a GAS course, accompanied by 2 N.C.O's.	
	17/7/16		No firing by own M.G's. 2 O.R's, 1 driver and 1 gunner, arrived from BASE.	
	18/7/16		In co-operation with raid by 18th Welsh Regt. 2 M.G's swept enemy parapet to right and left of the point where the raid took place. Other 4 M.G.'s fired on their communications with indirect fire. The enemy did not retaliate to any great extent.	
	19/7/16		No indirect fire was used, but 1 M.G. in the front line dispersed an enemy working party.	

Army Form C. 2118.

WAR DIARY
or
INTELLIGENCE SUMMARY

(Erase heading not required.)

Instructions regarding War Diaries and Intelligence Summaries are contained in F. S. Regs., Part II. and the Staff Manual respectively. Title Pages will be prepared in manuscript.

Place	Date	Hour	Summary of Events and Information	Remarks and references to Appendices
Les Brebis	July 20		Indirect fire was carried out on enemy trench starting at 5 p.m. Enemy replied on Coy. H.Q. and railway crossing at L.35.d.86 with shrapnel. No damage was done, but some men and horses had narrow escapes.	
	July 21 a.m.		Internal relief took place; 2/Lt. HERBERT and TURNER taking over SUPPORT and FRONT LINE guns; 2/Lt. HARKNESS relieved 2/Lt. ANDERTON with reserve guns. O.C. Coy. making arrangements with O.C. 120 Coy. for relief by that Coy. Complaint made by 12th S.W.B. that M.G. bullets were dropping into front line trenches investigated and proved incorrect.	
	July 21. p.m.		120th M.G. Coy. relieved 115th M.G. Coy. in all their positions. 2 guns of No. 2 section stayed in Z trench under Sgt. HARRIS.	
		21:00	Relief complete. All guns inspected; numerous spare parts missing, which will be charged to Section Officers.	
	July 23		Bathing parade in p.m. 2/Lt. BURCHETT, 2 N.C.O's and 20 men with 4 guns proceeded to LOOS, to report to O.C. LOOS defences.	
		21:00	Transport and men came under enemy M.G. fire on the LOOS - LENS road, but escaped without any casualties.	
	23 July		Church parade in a.m. O.C. Coy. proceeded to NOEUX-LES-MINES to see DADOS and SUPPLY OFFICER of 40th Divn.	

Army Form C. 2118.

WAR DIARY
or
INTELLIGENCE SUMMARY
(Erase heading not required.)

Instructions regarding War Diaries and Intelligence Summaries are contained in F. S. Regs., Part II. and the Staff Manual respectively. Title Pages will be prepared in manuscript.

Place	Date	Hour	Summary of Events and Information	Remarks and references to Appendices
Les Brebis	July 24	a.m.	Guns cleaned, and ordinary training carried out.	
		p.m.	Ordinary training.	
	July 25	a.m.	Route march by sections in full marching order.	
		p.m.	Ordinary M.G. training.	
	July 26	a.m.	Route march by sections in full marching order.	
		p.m.	M.G. training in p.m.	
	July 27	a.m.	2/Lt BURCHETT having been relieved by Lt. Pole, M.S. Coy at LOOS returned to Coy. Hqrs.	
			Route march by sections in full marching order; No 2 section overhauling guns.	
	July 28	a.m.	Route march in full marching order.	
			10 men attended gas demonstration.	
		p.m.	O.C. making arrangements with O.C. 120th M.G. Coy. to relief.	
	July 29	a.m.	The Coy. relieved the 120th Coy. in the new extended line.	
			2/Lt ANDERTON No 1 section in MG1, S1, S2, S3 frontline.	
			2/Lt BURCHETT No 2 " " MG8, S5, S6, S7 "	
			2/Lt HERBERT No 3 " " MG15, 17, S10, R21 "	
			2/Lt GROVES No 4 " " R1, R3, R.9, R11 "	
			2/Lt EDWARDES J.E. 15th R.W.F. was attached to this Coy., & posted to No 2 Section.	
	July 30	a.m.	Route march for men left behind.	
		2 p.m.	O.C. went round trenches occupied by No 1, 2, 3 sections. — Consulted with R.E. re dug-outs.	

Army Form C. 2118.

WAR DIARY
or
INTELLIGENCE SUMMARY

(Erase heading not required.)

Place	Date	Hour	Summary of Events and Information	Remarks and references to Appendices
LES BREBIS	July 31		Indirect fire was kept on enemy communications. 3 working parties sent to report to R.E. to complete dug-outs and work at S1, S2, S3. 3 Lewis Guns were moved to CALONNE defences. Weather has been warm for 2 days.	

A.S. Hartmann Capt.
O.C. 119th Bde M.G. Coy.

Army Form C. 2118.

119th M.G.Coy.
Vol 3

WAR DIARY
or
INTELLIGENCE SUMMARY
(Erase heading not required.)

Instructions regarding War Diaries and Intelligence Summaries are contained in F.S. Regs., Part II. and the Staff Manual respectively. Title Pages will be prepared in manuscript.

Place	Date	Hour	Summary of Events and Information	Remarks and references to Appendices
LES BREBIS	Aug. 1	9 p.m.	Indirect M.G. fire was used throughout the night, and during part of the day. #1 mule wounded with shrapnel.	
	Aug. 2		Internal relief carried out. 2/Lt. TURNER relieved 2/Lt. ANDERTON; 2/Lt. HARKNESS relieved 2/Lt. HERBERT. 2/Lt. EDWARDES (attached) went up to shares duties with 2/Lt. BURCHETT. The weather still remains very hot. Indirect fire carried out at night.	
	Aug. 3		The weather slightly cooler with same troops; indirect fire was carried out at night as usual.	
	Aug. 4		Indirect fire carried out at night.	
	Aug. 5		Internal relief carried out: 2/Lt. ANDERTON, 2/Lt. HERBERT, 2/Lt. GROVES, and 2/Lt. EDWARDES remaining in trenches. The R.E. working on new emplacement at S3 struck a loud odour for the team to hide in. Indirect fire carried out at night.	
	Aug. 7		The weather continues to be warm. Enemy shelled BETHUNE causing many casualties. Indirect fire carried out as usual.	
	Aug. 8		Vickers guns used indirect fire, and by night fired on O.P.s in enemy's wire. There was a Gas alarm at 11 p.m.	
	Aug. 9		Guns kept on firing at O.P.s in wire; 4 guns in MAROC SECTOR relieved.	
	Aug. 10		Internal relief took place; 2/Lt. TURNER, BURCHETT and GROVES remaining in trenches. 2 guns went to THE OUSELS; 2 guns of Reserve Bde. evacuated 2 Post.	

Army Form C. 2118.

WAR DIARY
or
INTELLIGENCE SUMMARY
(Erase heading not required.)

Instructions regarding War Diaries and Intelligence Summaries are contained in F. S. Regs., Part II. and the Staff Manual respectively. Title Pages will be prepared in manuscript.

Place	Date	Hour	Summary of Events and Information	Remarks and references to Appendices
LES BREBIS	Aug 11		Vickers Guns used indirect fire and fired on Copse in ruins. O.C. Coy proceeded to NOEUX LES MINES to attend conference at 16th Divn Hd Qrs re Front line M.G's and returned.	
	Aug 12		Vickers Guns fires in conjunction with raid by a detachment of 12th S.W.B. 1 gun fired on Copse in ruins till 10.30 p.m. At midnight artillery barrage started, and raid commenced. 4 MG's swept enemy's parapet on each side of point of entry. 2 MG's enfiladed their support line and communication trench. 6 MG's fired in points in CITÉ DE LA PLAINE. Firing ceased: 12th S.W.B. all returned with 1 prisoner wounded. The weather continues to be very warm.	
	Aug 13	12.30		
	Aug 14		The weather was chillier, and cooler with some rain.	
	Aug 15		The 120th M.G. Coy relieved the Coy. in trenches at 4 p.m. 4 guns of the Coy relieved 4 guns 120th M.G. Coy in CALONNE defences.	
	Aug 16		Bathing parade in a.m. Training carried out in p.m.	
	Aug 17		Route march in a.m. Training p.m.	
	Aug 18		Route march in a.m. Training p.m.	

Army Form C. 2118.

WAR DIARY
or
INTELLIGENCE SUMMARY

(Erase heading not required.)

Instructions regarding War Diaries and Intelligence Summaries are contained in F.S. Regs., Part II. and the Staff Manual respectively. Title Pages will be prepared in manuscript.

Place	Date	Hour	Summary of Events and Information	Remarks and references to Appendices
LES BREBIS	Aug 19		Route march a.m. Training p.m.	
	Aug 20		Church parade a.m. (for all denominations).	
	Aug 21		Inspection of Coy by Brig. Gen. C. CUNLIFFE OWEN. C.B. new G.O.C. 119th Infy Bde. Bathing parade for 25 men 5 – 6 p.m.	
	Aug 22		Route march a.m. Training p.m. for attached men. Weather has been cooler with some showers.	
	Aug 23	a.m.	O.C. Coy proceeded to MAZINGARBE to see O.C. 47th M.G. Coy re relief in sector. The relief took place; 10 guns going into the line as follows:– 6 RESERVE LINE, 2 in LOOS DEFENCES, 2 in LENS ROAD REDOUBT; 2/Lt GROVES & HARKNESS in trenches.	
		p.m.	O.C. proceeded to LOOS and return.	
	Aug 24		Training carried out at Coy HQ, ordinary training at Coy HQ reported.	
	Aug 25		O.C. proceeded to LOOS and return. Weather unsettled with rain, and trenches wet. LOOS very quiet.	
	Aug 26		O.C. proceeded to LOOS and return. Weather than the two previous days.	
	Aug 27		No. 1 Section (2 guns) relieved in LENS ROAD REDOUBT. O.C. proceeded to LOOS and return.	
	Aug 28		Internal relief took place; 2/Lt MACDONALD and HERBERT came to trenches. O.C. Coy and 2/Lt ANDERTON proceeded to LOOS and stayed in C.15 billet.	

Army Form C. 2118.

WAR DIARY
or
INTELLIGENCE SUMMARY

(Erase heading not required.)

Instructions regarding War Diaries and Intelligence Summaries are contained in F. S. Regs., Part II. and the Staff Manual respectively. Title Pages will be prepared in manuscript.

Place	Date	Hour	Summary of Events and Information	Remarks and references to Appendices
LES BREBIS	Aug 29		Weather very wet in p.m. Trenches in LOOS in bad condition.	
	Aug 30		O.C. Coy & 2/Lt ANDERTON proceeded to LES BREBIS to hold orderly room, and returned to LOOS.	
	Aug 31		O.C. Coy proceeded to LES BREBIS. A working party of 63 O.R. under 2/Lt. EDWARDES proceeded to LOOS to dig dug-outs under R.E. supervision.	

A. Mannon
Capt.

2449 Wt. W14957/M90 750,000 1/16 J.B.C. & A. Forms/C.2118/12.

WAR DIARY
or
INTELLIGENCE SUMMARY

(Erase heading not required.)

Army Form C. 2118.

119 M.G. Coy Vol 4

Place	Date	Hour	Summary of Events and Information	Remarks and references to Appendices
LES BREBIS	Sept.1		Internal relief took place at LOOS. 2/Lt. GROVES and HARKNESS going to trenches. Arg. carts for LEWIS gunners started under supervision of R.E.	
	Sept 2		Men at Coy HQ employed in improving billets.	
	" 3		O.C. proceeded to LOOS re enemy mine - The mine was blown near SEAFORTH CRATER by the enemy at 8 p.m. About 60 yards of front line trench was damaged -	
	" 4		O.C. returned from LOOS 4 a.m. Men engaged in improving billets at Coy HQ.	
	" 5		Internal Relief took place at LOOS 2/Lt MACDONALD, HERBERT going to trenches 2/Lt ANDERTON returned from LOOS	
	" 6		Men at Coy HQ engaged in improving billets	
	" 7		Men at Coy HQ engaged in General fatigues.	
	" 8		Indirect fire was carried out by 4 guns on the LOOS LENS road	
	" 9		Indirect fire was carried out by 6 guns on the road in LENS	
	" 10		The 121st M.G. Coy started to relieve the 119th M.G. Coy in the LOOS sector. 1 OR killed. 1 wounded	
	" 11		Relief complete by 4 a.m. Company employed in cleaning billets, and checking guns and spare parts.	

Army Form C. 2118.

WAR DIARY
or
INTELLIGENCE SUMMARY
(Erase heading not required.)

Instructions regarding War Diaries and Intelligence Summaries are contained in F. S. Regs, Part II. and the Staff Manual respectively. Title Pages will be prepared in manuscript.

Place	Date	Hour	Summary of Events and Information	Remarks and references to Appendices
LES BREBIS	Sept 12		Route march in a.m. Training carried on p.m.; paid the men in p.m.	
	Sept 13		Battalion parade a.m. Tactical scheme with whole company in p.m.	
	Sept 14		Ordinary training a.m. O.C. and 2/Lt. ANDERTON proceeded to 'B' series positions MAROC.	
	Sept 15		Company employed in training and in improving billets. 2/Lt. F.C. WAKE proceeded to ENGLAND on special leave.	
	Sept 16		Company training carried out; the attached men are now as good with the gun as the old M.G.C. men.	
	Sept 17		Church parade in a.m.	
	Sept 18		Coy. getting guns ready for relief in a.m. T.2/Lt BURCHETT promoted T.LIEUT. dated July 6.16 (Gazette Sept. 13.16).	
	Sept 18/19		The 115th Coy. relieved the 120th M.G. Coy. in the MAROC sector; relief complete about 3 a.m. 2/Lts. TURNER, HARKNESS, GRAVES and EDWARDS gun of Trenches. 2nd Lt D. MACDONALD promoted to temp. LIEUT. whilst acting as 2nd in command of a company dated April 20.15.16. LIEUT. D. MACDONALD proceeded to ENGLAND on leave.	
	Sept 19		Vickers guns fired on the LENS road at intervals, and on enemy searchlight.	
	Sept 20			
	Sept 21		Vickers guns carried out night firing on enemy communications	

Army Form C. 2118.

WAR DIARY
or
INTELLIGENCE SUMMARY
(Erase heading not required.)

Instructions regarding War Diaries and Intelligence Summaries are contained in F. S. Regs., Part II. and the Staff Manual respectively. Title Pages will be prepared in manuscript.

Place	Date	Hour	Summary of Events and Information	Remarks and references to Appendices
Sept. Les BREBIS	22.		Vickers Guns fired on the LENS road, and Colts in enemy wire.	
	23.		Vickers Guns fired on Colts in enemy wire.	
	24.		Vickers guns fired on LENS Rd. and Colts in wire; O.C. making arrangements with Infy. for Commandos re projected raid.	
	25.	9.15 pm	7th Welsh party started to raid enemy trenches; no enemy prisoner captured.	
			8 M.G.'s co-operated.	
	26.	10 pm	Gas alarm, which was found to be a mistake	
		12.30 am	12th S.W.B. raided enemy trenches, and encountered strong opposition; no identification was obtained.	
			8 M.G.'s co-operated.	
			Internal relief took place.	
	27.		M.G.'s fired on enemy roads and communications.	
	28.		2nd Lt. F.C. WAKE and LIEUT. D. MACDONALD returned from leave to ENGLAND.	
			M.G.'s carried out indirect fire on CITE ST. PIERRE roads.	
	29.		M.G.'s fired on Colts in wire, and roads at CITE DE LA PLAINE.	
	30.	10 p.m	18th Welsh raided enemy trenches; 9 M.G.'s co-operated; 1 Hun helmet was obtained.	

A.J. Harman
Capt.
a/s. 115th M.G. Coy

Army Form C. 2118.

119. M G C

Vol 8

WAR DIARY
or
INTELLIGENCE SUMMARY

(Erase heading not required.)

Instructions regarding War Diaries and Intelligence Summaries are contained in F. S. Regs., Part II. and the Staff Manual respectively. Title Pages will be prepared in manuscript.

Place	Date	Hour	Summary of Events and Information	Remarks and references to Appendices
LES BREBIS	Oct. 1		7 Vickers Guns co-operated in an unsuccessful raid by the 19th R.W.F. They were firing for an hour and a quarter.	
	Oct. 2.		The men in billets employed recovering the mule shelters.	
	Oct. 3.		2/Lt. J. TURNER proceeded to hospital sick; indirect fire was carried out.	
	Oct. 4.		Internal relief took place; 2/Lt. T. J. GROVES came back to billets. Our Guns fired an enemy roads and communications.	
	Oct. 5.		The ½ Coy. at rest improving billets and horse standings.	
	Oct. 6.		Vickers Guns fired an enemy roads and billets in CITÉ ST PIERRE and DE LA PLAINE	
	Oct. 7.		The half Coy. at rest improving billets.	
	Oct. 8.	a.m.	O.C. proceeded to trenches with O.C. 111th M.G. Coy re handing over 6 guns in the MAROC SECTOR. Church parade in a.m.	
		p.m.	6 guns co-operated with the 121st Bde. in a raid of enemy trenches.	

Army Form C. 2118.

WAR DIARY
or
INTELLIGENCE SUMMARY

(Erase heading not required.)

Instructions regarding War Diaries and Intelligence Summaries are contained in F.S. Regs., Part II. and the Staff Manual respectively. Title Pages will be prepared in manuscript.

Place	Date	Hour	Summary of Events and Information	Remarks and references to Appendices
LES BREBIS	Oct. 9	2 p.m.	The 111th M.G. Coy. relieved the 119th M.G. Coy. in 6 gun junkers. 2/Lt. ANDERTON and No. 1 section returned to Coy. HQ.; 2/Lt. BURCHETT returned to Coy. HQ. 2/Lt. GROVES relieves 2/Lt. HERBERT, who returned to V Coy. HQ. No. 2 + No. 3 sections; ½ no. 4 section returned to gun team of No. 4 section was attached to No. 1 gun team HQ. Battalion parade and overhauling guns, and improving billets.	
	Oct. 10			
	Oct. 11	3.30 a.m.	No. 1 section (2/Lt. ANDERTON) relieves 4 guns of the 121st M.G. Coy. in the ENCLOSURE LOOS. The new sector taken over is now known as the LOOS sector. Company at HQ improving billets.	
	Oct. 12		2/Lt. R. HARKNESS and 2 O.R.'s returned from CAMIÈRES M.G. SCHOOL. Internal relief; 2/Lt. BURCHETT returned to trenches vice 2/Lt. EDWARDS.	
	Oct. 13		2/Lt. HERBERT returned. 2/Lt. R. HARKNESS relieves 2/Lt. HERBERT in SOUTH ST.	
	Oct. 14		Church parade in c.m.	
	Oct. 15		Company at HQ improving billets.	
	Oct. 16		Two O.P.'s proceeds to M.G. School CAMIÈRES.	
	Oct. 17		Enemy bombarded sector heavily with TM's inflicting 3 casualties, slightly wounded.	
	Oct. 18		Company in billets working in stables.	
	Oct. 19		Enemy continued to live in S. JAMES KEEP. R26 gun was withdrawn to R23. 9 Vickers co-operated in raids of the 18th Welsh & 19th A.W.F.	

Army Form C. 2118.

WAR DIARY
or
INTELLIGENCE SUMMARY
(Erase heading not required.)

Instructions regarding War Diaries and Intelligence Summaries are contained in F. S. Regs., Part II. and the Staff Manual respectively. Title Pages will be prepared in manuscript.

Place	Date	Hour	Summary of Events and Information	Remarks and references to Appendices
LES BREBIS	Oct. 20.		Internal relief took place; 2/Lt. GROVES, 2/Lt. HERBERT, and 2/Lt. EDWARDS proceeding to Trenches.	
	Oct. 21		8 men per battalion permanently transferred to M.G.C. Other attached men will have to return to their units when the expected move takes place.	
	Oct. 22		2/Lt. J. EDWARDS 19th R.W.F. transferred to M.G.C. Indirect fire was carried out by 8 M.G's on enemy roads and billets.	
	Oct. 23.		Half company in billets engaged in improving billets.	
	Oct. 24		Half company in billets engaged in improving them. Heavy rain most of the day.	
	Oct. 25		3 officers of 73rd M.G. Coy. arrived; 2 proceeded round gun positions, the other inspected stables etc.	
	Oct. 26		Gun at 5J5 damaged by shell fire. Enemy very active. As there appeared to be a relief in enemy lines, indirect fire was carried out at night. Enemy quiet during the day.	
	Oct. 27		Another officer and O.C. 73rd M.G. Coy. were shewn round the LOOS SECTOR	

Army Form C. 2118.

WAR DIARY
or
INTELLIGENCE SUMMARY

(Erase heading not required.)

Place	Date	Hour	Summary of Events and Information	Remarks and references to Appendices
LES BREBIS	Oct. 28		The 73rd M.G. Coy relieved the Coy. in the line. Relief went very smoothly, and was complete by 10 p.m.	
	Oct. 29		Company engaged in cleaning up and refitting. 2/Lt MACDONALD and 2.O.R. proceeded to BRUAY to billet	
	Oct. 30		Company engaged in cleaning up, box respirators were tested in Gas-Chamber in p.m.	
	Oct. 31		Company packing limbers and preparing to move. Company left LES BREBIS 7 a.m. and proceeded via NOEUX LES MINES to BRUAY, arriving 11.30 a.m. Good billets in BRUAY.	

A.J. Harrison
Major

WAR DIARY.

119th M.G. Coy

Nov from 1st 1916
to
Nov. 30th 1916

Army Form C. 2118.

119 M.G. Coy

Vol 6

WAR DIARY
or
INTELLIGENCE SUMMARY

(Erase heading not required.)

Place	Date	Hour	Summary of Events and Information	Remarks and references to Appendices
BRUAY	Nov. 1	9 a.m.	The Company marched from billets en route for ORLENCOURT. The G.O.C. inspected the Coy. on the march.	
		1.30 pm	Arrived at ORLENCOURT. MAJOR A.L. HARRISON proceeded to ENGLAND on special leave.	
ORLENCOURT	2	9.30 a.m.	The Company left billets en route for PT. HOUVIN, arriving 1.15 p.m.	
PT. HOUVIN	3		Remained in billets and carried out training.	
	4	8 a.m.	Left billets and proceeded to ROUSEFAY arriving at 1.35 p.m.	
ROUSEFAY	5	8.30 a.m.	Left billets and marched to MONTISNY arriving 12 noon. Billets here very good.	
	6		Remained in billets and carried out training. Transport inspected by Army H.Q.	
MONTISNY	7		Weather very bad and rain interfered with training.	
	8		Rained all a.m. Tactical scheme carried out in p.m.	
	9	8.30 a.m.	Left MONTISNY and marched to GRIMONT arriving 10 a.m. Training carried out in p.m. MAJOR A.L. HARRISON rejoined from leave.	
GRIMONT				

Army Form C. 2118.

WAR DIARY
or
INTELLIGENCE SUMMARY
(Erase heading not required.)

Instructions regarding War Diaries and Intelligence Summaries are contained in F.S. Regs., Part II. and the Staff Manual respectively. Title Pages will be prepared in manuscript.

Place	Date	Hour	Summary of Events and Information	Remarks and references to Appendices
GRIMONT	10		Training carried out Firing on range in p.m.	
	11.		Training carried out Firing on range in p.m.	
	12		No church parade; firing on range in a.m. Rugby football match in p.m.	
	13.		Training carried out. Firing on the range in p.m.	
	14		Training carried out Firing in p.m.	
	15	10.45 a.m.	The Bn. left their billets and marched in the Brigade Column to WAVANS, arriving 2 p.m.	
	16		Training carried out in a.m. Firing in p.m.	
WAVANS	17		Left billets at 10 a.m. and marched to VILLERS L'HOPITAL arriving 11 a.m.	
VILLERS L'HOPITAL	18.		Left billets at 10.55 a.m. and marched to NEUVILLETTE, arriving 2 p.m.	
NEUVILLETTE	19.		Left billets at 10.30 a.m. and marched to LE SUICH arriving 11.30 a.m. LIEUT. T.H. BURCHETT and Pte. T.W. BRADLEY proceeded to ENGLAND on leave	

2449 Wt. W14957/M90 750,000 1/16 J.B.C. & A. Forms/C.2118/12.

Army Form C. 2118.

WAR DIARY
or
INTELLIGENCE SUMMARY
(Erase heading not required.)

Instructions regarding War Diaries and Intelligence Summaries are contained in F.S. Regs., Part II. and the Staff Manual respectively. Title Pages will be prepared in manuscript.

Place	Date	Hour	Summary of Events and Information	Remarks and references to Appendices
LE SUICH	20.		Training Carried out.	
	21.		Training Carried out. Weather very damp and cold.	
	22.		The Coy. left Liliers at 9 a.m. and marched to BEAUVAL arriving 12.45 p.m.	
BEAUVAL	23.		The Coy. left Liliers at 8.20 a.m. and marched to BARLETTE arriving 12.45 p.m.	
BARLETTE	24.		The Coy. left Liliers at 8.15 a.m. and marched to EPAGNE arriving @ 2.35 p.m.	
EPAGNE	25.		Men employed in kit inspection and cleaning kit; many suffer from sore feet and to had boots, which have worn out in 13 weeks.	
	26.		Training Carried out: Church Parade for non-Conformists in p.m.	
	27.		Training Carried out: firing in p.m.	
	28.		Training Carried out: firing stoppages in p.m.	
	29.		Training Carried out: firing in p.m.	
	30.		Physical drill and hosing in a.m. Firing in p.m.	

A.S. Hammond Major
C.J. 119th M.G. Coy.

WAR DIARY

of 119th Machine Gun Coy.

from Dec. 1. 16 to Dec. 31. 16.

Army Form C. 2118.

Instructions regarding War Diaries and Intelligence Summaries are contained in F.S. Regs., Part II. and the Staff Manual respectively. Title Pages will be prepared in manuscript.

WAR DIARY
or
INTELLIGENCE SUMMARY
(Erase heading not required.)

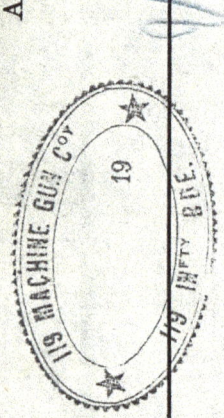

119 MACHINE GUN COY
119 INFTY BDE.

Vol 7

Place	Date	Hour	Summary of Events and Information	Remarks and references to Appendices
EPAGNE	Dec 1.16		Lt.-Col. R.G. CLARKE arrived 9.45 a.m. and inspected the Coy. and their work. Lt. J.H. BURCHETT and Pte. J.W. BRADLEY arrived from U.K. off leave. Firing in a.m. Company training in p.m.	
	2.		Company training in a.m. - Firing in p.m.	
	3.		Church parade 11 a.m. at EAUCOURT. O.C. and 4 other officers proceeded to near N. of BAVCAMPS to attend tactical scheme and meet XI Corps M.G. Officer, returning 2.30 p.m. Firing on range in p.m.	
	4.		Training carried out in a.m. - Firing on range in p.m.	
	5.		Training carried out.	
	6.		Training carried out.	
	7.		Training carried out: tactical scheme in p.m. - 1.O.R. from transport admitted hospital suffering from carbuncle - spinal meningitis.	
	8.		All transport men isolated. Unfit men examined by A.D.M.S. in p.m. at EAUCOURT - 10 men recommended for transfer to Base Depot.	
	9.		Inspection by G.O.C. 119th Infy Bde. 12 noon. Transport under 2/Lt. D.M. EVANS left for ST. SAUVEUR.	

Army Form C. 2118.

WAR DIARY
or
INTELLIGENCE SUMMARY
(Erase heading not required.)

Instructions regarding War Diaries and Intelligence Summaries are contained in F.S. Regs., Part II. and the Staff Manual respectively. Title Pages will be prepared in manuscript.

[Stamp: 119 MACHINE GUN COY / 119 INF^{TY} BDE.]

Place	Date	Hour	Summary of Events and Information	Remarks and references to Appendices
EPAGNE	10		The Coy. entrained at PONT REMY 7.30 a.m. and proceeded to EDGEHILL, arriving 12 noon, then marched to Camp 12 LES CELESTINS.	
LES CELESTINS	11		Transport arrived by road from ST. SAVEUR 7.30 p.m.	
	12		Coy. employed in cleaning up the camp, which was left filthy by the French.	
	13		Coy. training carried out; 1 section working cleaning up camp.	
	14		Coy. training carried out; 1 section drawing	
	15		Coy. training carried out; 1 section and finishing latrines.	
	16		Coy. training carried out; firing on 25 yds range in p.m. 1 section building baths and dressing	
	17		Coy. training carried out; improvements to camp carried on by 1 section.	
	18		Coy. training carried out; ½ Coy. attended church parade and ½ Coy. improving Company billeted in huts; camp.	
	19		Training carried out; firing in p.m. 1 section improving camp.	
	20		Training carried out; firing on range; 1 section improving camp.	
			Reinforcement of 12 O.R.'s arrived from base.	
			Training carried out; firing on range; 1 section improving camp.	

WAR DIARY
or
INTELLIGENCE SUMMARY

(Erase heading not required.)

Army Form C. 2118.

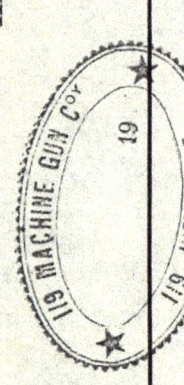

Place	Date	Hour	Summary of Events and Information	Remarks and references to Appendices
LES CELESTINS	21		Training carried out; firing in p.m.	
	22.		Training carried out; kit inspection in a.m. Firing in p.m. 1 section employed improving Camp.	
	23		Training carried out. Lt. J.A. BURCHETT proceeded to the 98th M.G. Coy near RANCOURT to O.C. Coy. The new front returning 11.30 p.m. – very stormy weather.	
	24		Reconnoitre in a.m. All sections bathed in waterproof sheets in huts. Church parade in a.m. Xmas day, and held a concert in the evening. The men kept this day as Xmas day. SAA all day.	
	25		Men engaged in packing limbers, wagons etc all day.	
	26		O.C. Coy. and Lt. BURCHETT left at 7 a.m. and proceeded to LE FORÊT to make arrangements re relieving 98th M.G. Coy. Lt. BURCHETT stayed in trenches and reconnoitred the front line at pres. H.Q at BRAY and thence to Camp 17 near SUZANNE. G.C. Coy. returned to Camp 17 with Lt. ANDERTON.	
Camp 17 SUZANNE	27		The Coy marched to MAUREPAS in motor lorries to relieve 98th M.G. Coy's. The Coy proceeded to MAUREPAS via COMMÈLES to LE PRIEZ FARM; 1 O.R. killed & 1 O.R. They marched from MAUREPAS. Lt. BURCHETT was wounded. Relief complete by 9.30 p.m. dangerously wounded. Transport moved to Camp 21 with Lieut. MACDONALD. Details left behind moved to MAUREPAS and 5 Gun teams at LE FORÊT; 5 Gun teams mmth O.C. Coy's H.Q. Lt. HERBERT engaged in anti-aircraft work.	

WAR DIARY
or
INTELLIGENCE SUMMARY

(Erase heading not required.)

Army Form C. 2118.

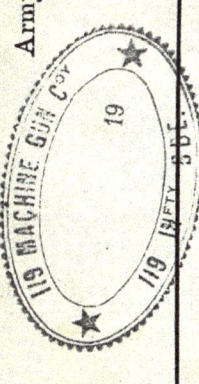

Place	Date	Hour	Summary of Events and Information	Remarks and references to Appendices
LE FORET	28.		O.C. Coy inspected recent line in p.m. 2/Lt. HARKNESS arrived to take the place of Lt. BURCHETT from Camp 21.	
	29		2/Lt. HERBERT relieved Lieut. ANDERTON in the front line system - 1 gun team could not be found & was not relieved 2/Lt. EDWARDS.	
	30.		Sgt. PARKER'S gun team relieved and placed under G.S.O. 1 in a.m. O.C. proceeded round recent line with G.S.O. 1 in p.m. Lt. Col Clarke M.G.O. XIV Corps arrived in p.m.	
	31.		O.C. proceeded to RANCOURT at 5 a.m. reconnoitring new gun positions returning 10 p.m. Lieut ANDERTON relieved Lieut. HERBERT in front line system.	

R.J.Hammorow
Major
O/c 119 M.G. Coy

Army Form C. 2118.

WAR DIARY
or
INTELLIGENCE SUMMARY
(Erase heading not required.)

119 M G Coy   Vol 8

Instructions regarding War Diaries and Intelligence Summaries are contained in F.S. Regs., Part II. and the Staff Manual respectively. Title Pages will be prepared in manuscript.

Place	Date	Hour	Summary of Events and Information	Remarks and references to Appendices
LE FORÊT	Jan 1/17		Lt. Col. CLARKE, Comdr M.G. Officer proceed reconnoitring trenches with O.C. Coy 5.30 a.m. New supports for guns positions chosen.	
	2		O.C. reconnoitred trenches at 5.30 a.m. O.C. 241st Coy arrived to reconnoitre. 2/Lt. HERBERT relieved from duty from the Base. 2/Lt. LORDEN arrived making shelters for new positions, all guns moved by 11 p.m. Guns teams en/3rds in Command of 120th Coy arrived to reconnoitre and make arrange-	
	3		2 officers and O.C. Coy reconnoitred trenches with 12 m.g./hr. ments for relief of 119th Coy in the RANCOURT sector.	
	4		120th Coy relieved the 119th Coy in Loan - march to Camp 17. The 119 M.G. Coy proceeds by lorry (or motor). CAPT. (?) VENABLES reported in Common Camp. Day spent in Common Camp	
Camp 17	5.		Company at work improving huts and on parade. Lieut. G.E.A. ANDERTON & 2/Lt. R. HARKNESS reported sick.	
	6.		Company getting ready for trenches. 121st M.G.C. O.C. and CAPT. VENABLES proceeds to ANGUSTURA re relieving in BUCHAVESNES sector	
	7.		Company relieved 121st M.G. Coy in BOUCHAVESNES sector	
BOUCHAVESNES	8.		Quiet-Herbert reconnoitred trenches	
	9			

WAR DIARY or INTELLIGENCE SUMMARY

Army Form C. 2118.

(Erase heading not required.)

Instructions regarding War Diaries and Intelligence Summaries are contained in F. S. Regs., Part II. and the Staff Manual respectively. Title Pages will be prepared in manuscript.

Place	Date	Hour	Summary of Events and Information	Remarks and references to Appendices
BOUCHAVESNES	Jan 10		LIEUT. D. MACDONALD proceeded to O.R. & struck off strength of company	
	11		2 LIEUT SPURRELL relieved 2 LIEUT LORDEN in front line position	
			LIEUT HERBERT engaged in fixing gun position	
	12		C.O. inspected 25th & evacuated to Field Ambulance.	
			CAPT VENABLES assumed command of the company	
			2 LIEUT LORDEN relieved 2 LIEUT SPURRELL in front line position	
	13		C.O. reconnoitred front line position with LIEUT. HERBERT at 4 P.M.	
	14		2 LIEUT SPURRELL relieved 2 LIEUT LORDEN in front line position.	
	15		C.O., Lieut HERBERT & 2 LIEUT LORDEN visited front line.	
			Gun still fired on to ANDOVER for ½ hour.	
	16		C.O. reconnoitred ground for gun positions in intermediate line with Brigade Major.	
	17		C.O. & 2 LIEUT DEXTER upstirrup pumps for fire Reserve guns	
			2 LIEUT O.P. DUNN reconnoitred gun position at CANIERS.	
	18		12:05 M.G. Bay relieved 11/15th M.G. Bay in BOUCHAVESNES sector	
			11/15 M.G. Bay proceeded by march along to Camp 17	
			2 LIEUT R. HARKNESS returned from hospital.	
Camp 17	19		Day operation cleaning up.	
	20		Company at work improving roads etc.	
			MAJOR A.L. HARRISON returned from hospital.	
	21		Company had baths at Camp 21.	
			Company interned for benches.	
			Capt. VENABLES & LIEUT. HERBERT proceeded to RANCOURT re relieving 12/13 M.G. Bay in the sector.	

Army Form C. 2118.

WAR DIARY
or
INTELLIGENCE SUMMARY

(Erase heading not required.)

Instructions regarding War Diaries and Intelligence Summaries are contained in F.S. Regs., Part II. and the Staff Manual respectively. Title Pages will be prepared in manuscript.

Place	Date	Hour	Summary of Events and Information	Remarks and references to Appendices
Camp 17	Jan 22		The 119th M.G. Coy relieved the 121st M.G. Coy in the RANCOURT sector. Lt. EDWARDS and No. 2 section relieved the Support Guns. 2/Lt. LORDEN and No. 1 " " Reserve " 2/Lt. HERBERT and No. 3 " " Coy's line " 2/Lt. DUNN and No. 4 " remained in Coy Reserve. Capt. VENABLES stayed at advanced Coy. H.Q. MAJOR HARRISON stayed at LE FORÊT.	
LE FORÊT	Jan 23		Enemy heavily shelled line near advanced Coy. H.Q. Casualties 4 O.R. killed, 2 wounded and 2 guns buried in a dug out, an enemy aeroplane came down in flames at LE FORÊT.	
	-24		Lt. HERBERT and No. 3 section relieved Lt. EDWARDS and No. 2 section.	
	-25		Officers of 25th M.G. Coy arrived to make arrangements re relief. O.C. proceeded to RANCOURT in p.m. and visited Support - Reserve line Coys.	
	26.		1 officer of 25th M.G. Coy arrived at advanced Coy. H.Q. and stayed to reconnoitre the support line Coys. A/Adjt. Major proceeded to No. 1 of RANCOURT to reconnoitre a strong point. O.C. Coy. + A/Adjt. Major proceeded to No. 1 of RANCOURT to reconnoitre a strong point.	
	27		The 25th M.G. Coy relieved the 119th M.G. Coy in the RANCOURT sector.	
Camp 12	28		The 119th M.G. Coy proceeded by march routes to Camp 12, SAILLY-LAURETTE, arriving 10 P.M.	
	29.		Day spent in cleaning up. Inspection by O.C. Coy.	
	30.		Day spent in general training & cleaning him Lewis gun equipment. Officers hut destroyed by fire at 3 A.M. Any amount of kit lost. Major HARRISON admitted to hospital. Capt. VENABLES assumed command of company.	

Army Form C. 2118.

WAR DIARY
or
INTELLIGENCE SUMMARY
(Erase heading not required.)

Instructions regarding War Diaries and Intelligence Summaries are contained in F. S. Regs., Part II. and the Staff Manual respectively. Title Pages will be prepared in manuscript.

Place	Date	Hour	Summary of Events and Information	Remarks and references to Appendices
CAMP 12	31 Jan		Company employed in General Training. 2 Lieut. DUNN admitted to Hospital.	

Blewitt Capt.
O.C. 118 M.T. Coy

Army Form C. 2118.

WAR DIARY
or
INTELLIGENCE SUMMARY. 119 M G Coy
(Erase heading not required.)

For 9

Instructions regarding War Diaries and Intelligence Summaries are contained in F. S. Regs., Part II. and the Staff Manual respectively. Title Pages will be prepared in manuscript.

Place	Date	Hour	Summary of Events and Information	Remarks and references to Appendices
Camp 12	1st Oct		Day spent in General Training.	
	2		Day spent in General Training. Capt. VENABLES, Lieut. EDWARDS & Cadet LORDEN attended Anti-Aircraft Demonstration	
	3		Half Holiday. Triangular Range in morning.	
	4		Company Bathed.	
	5		Lumber Cleaning.	
	6		General Training & Lumber Cleaning.	
	7		General Training	
	8		General Training	
	9		Capt. VENABLES went to LE FORÊT to arrange relief with 25th M.G. Coy.	
	10		Major HARRISON returned from hospital	
Camp 14	11		Company proceeded by march to Camp 17. Lieut. J. E. PRICE reported for duty.	
RANCOURT	12		119 M.G. Coy relieved 25 M.G. Coy in RANCOURT Sector.	
	13		RANCOURT heavily shelled in the evening. British Artillery Bombardment for 1½ hours. Various targets engaged with Indirect Fire	
	14		RANCOURT heavily barraged at dawn, in reply to British Artillery Bombardment. Major HARRISON proceeded on leave to U.K. Captain VENABLES assumed command of the company	
	15		Enemy trenches engaged with Indirect Fire. British Artillery Bombardment. Enemy has been engaged with Indirect Fire. British Artillery bombarded RANCOURT.	

WAR DIARY
or
INTELLIGENCE SUMMARY

(Erase heading not required.)

Army Form C. 2118.

Place	Date	Hour	Summary of Events and Information	Remarks and references to Appendices
RANCOURT	1916			
	16		2nd Lieut J.E. PRICE relieved 2nd Lieut EDWARDS in support line.	
	17		119 M.G. Coy relieved two A.A. guns of 121st M.G. Coy in LE FORÊT, for the day. Enemy position engaged with indirect fire.	
	18		Capt VENABLES & Lieut HERBERT reconnoitred positions for M.G. positions. Enemy discovered during the reconnaissance & engaged with direct fire.	
	19		Capt VENABLES & 2nd Lieut HERBERT reconnoitred positions for 3 A.A. Lewis guns.	
	20		Capt VENABLES & 2nd Lieut HARKNESS went to RANDOVER (BOUCHAVESNES Sector). Barrage rifle/anti 10th M.G. Coy	
	21		121st M.G. Coy relieved 119 M.G. Coy in Rainenville & Rue & AA position at LE FORÊT. 119th M.G. Coy relieved 18 M.G. Coy in ROSE & RUPERT (BOUCHAVESNES Sector). Heavy bombardment by both sides all along the sector, at 6 P.M.	
	22		119 M.G. Coy relieved in RANCOURT Sector by 121 M.G. Coy. 119 M.G. Coy proceeded by march to Camp III. Six guns were left at RANCOURT & LE FORÊT — 4 under 2nd Lieut DEXTER in Rainenville line & two under Lieut PRICE on A.A. Duty. Three guns were posted at BRAY under Lieut EDWARDS for A.A. duty.	
Camp III	23		Day spent in cleaning up & general fatigues.	
	24		Day spent in general training.	
	25		Day spent in general training.	
	26		2nd Lieut HARKNESS gazetted Lieutenant. Day spent in drill & training.	
	27		Major HARRISON returned from leave. Lieut HARKNESS relieved Lieut EDWARDS on A.A. duty at BRAY. Day spent in general training & fatigues. Capt VENABLES visited guns at RANCOURT & LE FORÊT.	
	28		Day spent in general training & fatigues. 2nd Lieut DUNN returned from hospital.	

Newenham Capt
for Major
O.C. 119 M.G. Coy

119 MACHINE GUN Coy

Army Form C. 2118.

WAR DIARY
or
INTELLIGENCE SUMMARY.
(Erase heading not required.)

Vol 10

119th M.G. Coy.

From March 1 - March 31. 1917

Army Form C. 2118.

WAR DIARY
or
INTELLIGENCE SUMMARY.
(Erase heading not required.)

Place	Date	Hour	Summary of Events and Information	Remarks and references to Appendices
Camp III GROVETOWN	March 1		Company carried out training and provided working party.	
	2		Company carried out training and provided working party. Capt VENABLES proceeded to RANCOURT and returned. O.C. Coy. proceeded to ETINGHEM and returned.	
	3		Company carried out training and provided working party. O.C. Coy proceeded to BRAY and returned.	
	4		Company carried out training and provided working party.	
	5		Company carried out training in huts owing to heavy snow and provided working party. Capt VENABLES proceeded to CLERY to arrange details of relief of the 19th M.G. Coy. Lt. J.E. EDWARDS proceeded to RANCOURT re relief of guns in Corps dump by guns of the 121st M/y Bde and returned. 2/Lt P.W. DEXTER relieved by guns of the 121st M/y Bde. arrived with his section 6 p.m.	
	6		Company training carried out. O.C. Coy and Lt. E.G. HERBERT proceeded to CLERY and returned. Lt J.E. PRICE and Lt R. HARKNESS relinquished their A.A. positions at LE FORET and BRAY and returned with their gun teams to Camp III.	
	7		Company engaged in preparing for Trenches O.C. inspected the Company at 2 p.m.	

Army Form C. 2118.

WAR DIARY
or
INTELLIGENCE SUMMARY.
(Erase heading not required.)

Instructions regarding War Diaries and Intelligence Summaries are contained in F. S. Regs., Part II. and the Staff Manual respectively. Title pages will be prepared in manuscript.

Place	Date	Hour	Summary of Events and Information	Remarks and references to Appendices
Camp III GROVETOWN	8		Company left 1 p.m. and proceeded to Camp 19 near SUZANNE	
Camp 19	9		Company left Camp 19 at 1 p.m. and relieved the 19th M.G. Coy. in the CLERY SECTOR	
	10		Company in Trenches – O.C. inspected front line and altered lines of fire	
CLERY	11		Company in Trenches. O.C. proceeded to CLERY CHATEAU.	
	12		Company in Trenches. Capt. VENABLES proceeded to SARMON FARM	
	13		Indirect fire was carried out on enemy lines and communications. O.C. and Capt. VENABLES reconnoitred the banks of RIVER SOMME near OMMIECOURT with a view to patrolling the island	
	14		O.C. Capt. VENABLES and 6 gun teams proceeded to positions near SARMON FARM. Barrage fire was opened at 10.30 p.m. and at 10.33 p.m. Capt. VENABLES attempted to cross the river in a boat, which stuck in the mud. No casualties occurred and no hostile retaliation was experienced.	
	15		121st M.G. Bty. (our M.G. Coy.) relieved the 115th M.G. Bty.	
	16		121st M.G. Coy. relieved the 119th M.G. Coy.	
Camp 17 SUZANNE	17		The Company arrived at Camp 17 9 a.m., and cleaned kit etc.	
	18		Church Parade. C of E. 11 a.m. Non-Conformist 6.00 p.m. 2/Lt. LORDEN and SPURRELL returned from M.G. School, CAMIERS.	

Army Form C. 2118.

WAR DIARY
or
INTELLIGENCE SUMMARY.

(Erase heading not required.)

Instructions regarding War Diaries and Intelligence Summaries are contained in F.S. Regs., Part II. and the Staff Manual respectively. Title pages will be prepared in manuscript.

Place	Date	Hour	Summary of Events and Information	Remarks and references to Appendices
Camp 17 SUZANNE	March 19		The Company marched from Camp 17 to CURLU. Capt. VENABLES and Lt. HERBERT proceeded to BOUCHAVESNES re relief of 120th M.G. Coy. and returned.	
CURLU	20.		The Company relieved the 120th Coy. in the BOUCHAVESNES Sector occupying positions in the old German lines. All guns were brought up in on pack mules.	
HAUT ALLAINES	21.		The Company advanced to HAUT ALLAINES arriving with transport 2 p.m. The roads were badly cut up by shell fire - O.C. reconnoitred last of resistance in a.m. Lts. HERBERT and EDWARDS with their sections occupied line MONT ST. QUENTIN - HAUT ALLAINES - AIZECOURT LE HAUT - MIDINETTE trench in p.m.	
AIZECOURT LE HAUT	22		The Company advanced to AIZECOURT LE HAUT making that village H.Q. Lt. PRICE and his section occupied a line BLUE COPSE - AIZECOURT - DRIANCOURT now joining up with Lt. RAMFATS - Lt. HERBERT and section rejoined the Company. O.C. reconnoitred new line of resistance with O.C. & M/G. Battalions. Corps M.G.O. arrived.	
	23		The Company were employed in digging emplacements for new line DRIANCOURT - TEMPLEUX LA FOSSE - GUJALU WOOD and completed them.	
	24		The Company engage enemy aeroplanes in AIZECOURT LE HAUT; the Coy. proceed back to BOUCHAVESNES to build roads.	
	25.		The Company attempted to improve their billets and horse standings.	
BOUCHAVESNES	26			
	27		The Company were making roads - Weather was miserable.	

Army Form C. 2118.

WAR DIARY
or
INTELLIGENCE SUMMARY.
(Erase heading not required.)

Instructions regarding War Diaries and Intelligence Summaries are contained in F. S. Regs., Part II. and the Staff Manual respectively. Title pages will be prepared in manuscript.

Place	Date	Hour	Summary of Events and Information	Remarks and references to Appendices
BOUCHAVESNES.	March 28		The Company were engaged in making roads	
	29.		The Company were engaged in making roads	
	30.		The Company were engaged in making roads. Tactical exercise was carried out by half the officers near PERONNE.	
	31.		The Company were engaged in making roads. Tactical exercise was carried out by half the officers near MOISLAINS.	

A Hermon
Major
Cyt. 119th M G Coy

Vol XI

WAR DIARY.

FOR

119TH M.G. COY.

FOR APRIL 1917.

119th M.G.C. Coy

Army Form C. 2118.

WAR DIARY
or
INTELLIGENCE SUMMARY.
(Erase heading not required.)

Instructions regarding War Diaries and Intelligence Summaries are contained in F. S. Regs., Part II. and the Staff Manual respectively. Title pages will be prepared in manuscript.

Places	Date	Hour	Summary of Events and Information	Remarks and references to Appendices
BOUCHAVESNES	April 1		The Company engaged in making roads. O.C. Coy 2Lt HERBERT. 2/Lts LORDEN and SPURRELL proceeded on a tactical exercise	
	2.		The Company engaged in making roads. Lt HERBERT and 2/Lt SPURRELL proceeded to ETRICOURT to guide Brigade. No. 3 Section under Coy. H.Q.	
	3.		The Company engaged in making roads and building gun pits. O.C. Coy 2Lts PRICE, EDWARDS and HARKNESS reconnoitred the NURLU – EQUANCOURT line of resistance to be occupied in case of necessity, returning via ETRICOURT.	
	4.		The Company engaged in making roads and gun pits. Snow – Snow all day –	
	5.		The Company engaged in making roads. O.C. Coy 2Lt PRICE. EDWARDS and HARKNESS reconnoitred the NURLU – EQUANCOURT line	
	6.		The Company engaged in preparing to move.	
	7.		The Company left 7.15 a.m. and marched to ETRICOURT arriving 7.15 a.m. Sections engaged in cleaning huts and limbers. 2/Lt J.E EDWARDS proceeded on leave to U.K.	
ETRICOURT	8.		1 section of the Company engaged in A.A. work. (Rifles with A.A. sights. New draft of 10 men arrived.) 3 Section Company training. All guns in Command	
	9.		1 section engaged in A.A. work. 2 sections engaged in firing. Firing on the range in p.m. 2/Lt J.E. PRICE proceeded to the 94th M.G. Coy. as 2nd in Command. 2/Lt E.G. HERBERT proceeded on leave to U.K.	

A5834. Wt. W4973 M687 750,000 8/16 D. D. & L. Ltd. Forms/C.2118/13.

Army Form C. 2118.

WAR DIARY
or
INTELLIGENCE SUMMARY.
(Erase heading not required.)

Map Ref 57c S.E. 1/20,000

Instructions regarding War Diaries and Intelligence Summaries are contained in F.S. Regs., Part II. and the Staff Manual respectively. Title pages will be prepared in manuscript.

Place	Date	Hour	Summary of Events and Information	Remarks and references to Appendices
ETANCOURT	10.		1 section engaged in A.A. work.	
			2 sections training.	
	11.		1 section working party / sub. section and left 5 p.m. and proceeded to FINS reporting to O.C. 121st M.G. Coy.	
			2/Lt. LORDEN and sub. section left 5 p.m. and proceeded to FINS reporting to O.C. 121st M.G. Coy	
			1 section engaged in A.A. work	
	12.		1 section training	
			1 section working party	
			1 section working party. FINS - YTRES line of resistance.	
			O.C. Coy. reconnoitred FINS - YTRES line of resistance.	
			2/Lt. LORDEN and sub. section rejoined company at 2.30 a.m. from FINS.	
	13.		1 section engaged in A.A. work	
			2 sections training	
			1 section working party	
			O.C. Coy. and 2/Lt. HARKNESS reconnoitred FINS - YTRES line; reconnaissance impeded by heavy snow.	
	14.		1 section engaged on A.A. work.	
			1 section working party.	
			2 sections training.	
	15.		1 section engaged on A.A. work.	
			1 section working party.	
			2 sections working party on FINS - YTRES line	
			O.C. Coy. visited FINS - YTRES line	
			1 section engaged on A.A. work.	
			1 section working party.	
			2 sections working party on FINS - YTRES line.	
	16.		CAPT. VENABLES C. proceeded to join 1/15 London Regt.	
			LIEUT. ROBINSON F.V. and LIEUT. ANDERTON G.E.A. arrived from M.G.C. Base Depot.	
			O.C. Coy visited FINS - YTRES line	
			1 section engaged on A.A. work	
			1 section working party	
			2 sections working party FINS - YTRES line	

Map Ref: 57c SE 1/20000

Army Form C. 2118.

WAR DIARY
or
INTELLIGENCE SUMMARY.
(Erase heading not required.)

Instructions regarding War Diaries and Intelligence Summaries are contained in F. S. Regs., Part II. and the Staff Manual respectively. Title pages will be prepared in manuscript.

Place	Date	Hour	Summary of Events and Information	Remarks and references to Appendices
ÉTRICOURT	17th	5 p.m.	No. 1 Section proceeded to relieve 1 Section of the 25th M.G.C. & N.E. of GOUZEAUCOURT. No. 4 Section & 2 P. 2 proceeded to relieve front of 120th M.G.C. in FINS-GOUZEAU- COURT WOOD LINE (MAIN LINE OF RESISTANCE). No. 3 Section proceeded to FINS to do Anti-Aircraft work. O.C. B Coy reconnoitred GOUZEAUCOURT Sector.	
FINS.	18.		2½ Sections in the line as on 17th. 1 Section A.A. work.	
		9 a.m.	H.Q. moved to FINS at 9 a.m.	
		2 p.m.	O.C. 6th & 2nd I/c reconnoitred GOUZEAUCOURT Sector.	
	19.		Sections in line as for 17th. 1 Section in A.A. work. ½ Section working party. O.C. 6th & 2nd I/c reconnoitred. 1 Section. By Front Line. 1½ Sections in Main Line of Resistance. No. 3 Section ½ of No. 2 Section moved up to the line.	
	20th	4.20 a.m.	At dawn the 6th & 4 lea 1½ Section co-operated with the 119th Inf. Bde. in an attack on Q24B9.07.5- FIFTEEN RAVINE- R20Q10.00- The Pard road exclusive. Gun positions were:- No. 1 Section 2 guns Q30 B.2.5. covering R26B-R21C. 2 guns under Lt. LORDEN Q24c26 to advance to Q30 B.2.5.- over FIFTEEN RAVINE No. 3 Section 3 guns Q30.c.95.50. Q30 D.12 covering from R13D8.1 to R26B ½ " 2 " 3 guns covered R13 D 8.2 to R.13 centrel	

Map Ref. 57cSE 2 vers 3 A

Army Form C. 2118.

WAR DIARY
or
INTELLIGENCE SUMMARY.

(Erase heading not required.)

Instructions regarding War Diaries and Intelligence Summaries are contained in F. S. Regs., Part II. and the Staff Manual respectively. Title pages will be prepared in manuscript.

Place	Date	Hour	Summary of Events and Information	Remarks and references to Appendices
FINS	APRIL 20		Operations continued. The attack was completely successful, FIFTEEN RAVINE was taken & the new line consolidated. 2 gun invs 2 LORD'N reached their position & advanced into FIFTEEN RAVINE. LINE Q24B 9775 – FIFTEEN RAVINE – R20.10.00. – L8 Pave moved becomes NEW FRONT LINE of 119th Inf Bde.	
"	21.		2 gun of 292 Section withdrawn from FIFTEEN RAVINE to FINS. L DEXTER (agy) reduced 2 guns of 921 Section reused FRONT LINE NE of GOUZ- EAUCOURT. No 3 Section occupied positions Q30D.05.20 Q30 55 P30Q4 2	
"	22.		6th HQ moved to GOUZEAUCOURT.	
GOUZEAU- COURT	23.	12am	No 1 Section moved its GOUZEAUCOURT H.M. 9 strongpoint at FINS	
"			92.4 Section & 292 Section relieved by 121 MG 6 in FINS – GOUZEAUCOURT. Wood line & proceeded to GOUZEAUCOURT. O.C. 6th reconnoitred the line.	
"	24th	4/15 a.m.	ATTACK. The 6th "co-operated with the 119th Inf Bde in an attack on frontier R19 A07 to R14 B18 (inclusive VILLERS PLOUICH) Position of guns. 4 in Reserve in SUNKEN RP NE GOUZ EI 4" high ground R16 A+B. 9 at central Gun Reserve	

A.5834 Wt.W4973-M687 750,000 8/16 D. D. & L. Ltd. Forms/C.2118/13.

WAR DIARY
INTELLIGENCE SUMMARY

Army Form C. 2118.

Trench Rd 5ye SE 1/25000

Place	Date	Hour	Summary of Events and Information	Remarks and references to Appendices
GOUZEAU-COURT.	APRIL 24		**OPERATIONS CONTD** A full description of these operations, a copy of O.C 119 R.G.B 24 orders, comments & a rough strong gun positions are attached. The operations were successful & all objectives taken.	A
"	25th		The LINE R19 A.07 - R14 B 18 became the NEW FRONT LINE. O.C. 6" reconnoitred new front line.	
"	26th		2 guns under LT EDWARDS moved to R14 C 39 covering VILLERS PLOUICH 2 guns under LT ANDERTON moved to FRONTLINE about R14 central 2 guns " LT LORDEN " R20 A 9.8 2 guns " LT HARKNESS " R20 b.6.4 + R G B 5.6 Stokes + gun emplacements improved	
"	27		LT HARKNESS proceeded on leave to U.K. to arrive 30th	
"	28		Much aerial activity. Several places fired on	
"	29.		2 casualties. 1 officer 2 LT SPURREL H W. 10 R 22 4567 PTE 1/12 CLEMENT slightly wounded by shrapnel. Both casualties proceeded to advanced dressg FIFTEEN RAVINE. No 1 section + No 2 Section relieved by 121 M.G. Coy.	
"	30th		No 1 & 2 Sections proceeded to F.M.S. number LT ANDERTON " FIFTEEN RAVINE " FRONTLINE R20 A 7.8.	

O.Hammann
for O.C. 119 M.G.C.Cy

APPENDIX A

119th Infantry Brigade.

Attached please find copy of orders for my Coy. for tomorrow, and map. The blue lines show my lines of fire; the yellow ground dangerous to our troops, while it is dark.

I am now proceeding to inform battalion commanders about this.

April 23rd 1917. (Sd) A.L.Harrison, Major,
Commdg. 119th M. G. Company.

ORDERS FOR APRIL 24th, 1917.   119th M.G.Coy.

Issued April 23rd 1917.   Ref. map 57.c.S.E. Edn. 3.A.

1. The 119th Infantry Bde. will assault the enemy position from R.19.a,0.7. to R.14.b.1.8. on 24th inst. The order of battle will be :-
   Right Battalion   18th Welsh.
   Left   ,,   17th Welsh.
   Support   R. W. Fus.
   Reserve   S. W. B.

2. The right battalion will obtain their objectives during darkness, and no opposition is expected on their front. On the left opposition is expected.

3. The 119th M. G. Coy. will assist with direct overhead fire.

4. Positions are allotted as follows :-
   No. 1 Section - In old front line (RESERVE)
   No. 3 Section - High ground R.26.a.& b.
   No. 2 & 4 ,,   - High ground Q.24.central.

5. The guns of Nos. 2,3. and 4 Sections will be dug in tonight and camouflaged, assisted by an infantry working party.

6. Duties of sections are as follows :-

   No. 1 - Defence of old front line; they will not move unless directly ordered by G.O.C. 119th Infantry Brigade, or O. C. Company.

   Nos 2 & 4, will fire on the valley running from R.3.d.10.00 to LA VACQUERIE as follows :-
       ZERO   strong point R.3.d.10.00. Range 1700^x
       ZERO + 6   Lift to 2000^x
       ZERO + 16   Lift to 2200^x
       ZERO + 26   Lift to 2500^x
       ZERO + 36   Lift to 2700^x

The O. C. 17th Welsh (left battalion) will call for assistance from No. 2 Section, if required, who will advance if ordered to do so. These guns will not traverse, but fire on the lines pointed out to them.

   No. 3. -   Will fire from R.26.a.& b. as follows :-
       ZERO   On VILLERS PLOUICH; on no account must they fire further west than 335° true bearing.
       ZERO + 6   Move 10° Right.
       ZERO + 26   Move another 10° Right.
       ZERO + 46   Move another 10° Right.
       ZERO + 56   Move another 10° Right.

Combined sights from 1700^x will be used.
   to 2000^x

7. As soon as it is daylight, section officers will see the situation from their positions, and issue orders accordingly. The M.G. safety angles for overhead fire will then be used.

8. The 2nd in command is responsible for S.A.A., rations and water supply.

9. Coy. H.Q. for the operation will be FIFTEEN RAVINE near O.C., 17th Welsh; telephones will be laid from R.26.a.0.8. and Q.24. central to Coy. H.Q.

Communications.

Each section will detail 4 runners who will proceed to FIFTEEN RAVINE from their Sections by 2. a.m. April 24th 1917. Of these, 2 will remain at Coy. H.Q. and 2 return to their sections.

Section Officers are reminded that communication must be maintained with Coy. H.Q. <u>at all costs,</u> and runners must be instructed to proceed direct to Coy. H.Q. in spite of enemy fire.

As section officers will be in commanding positions their reports must show the position of our infantry, and other details of importance, which may not directly concern them.

(Sd) A.L. Harrison, Major,

Commanding 119th M. G. Company.

119th Machine Gun Coy.

REPORT ON THE ACTION OF APRIL 24th, 1917 near VILLERS PLOUICH.

Ref.map 57.c.S.E.
Edn. 3.A.

The company co-operated with the infantry and O.C.Coy remained in close communication with O.C. 17th Welsh Regt. in FIFTEEN RAVINE during the action, as opposition was expected on his left flank.

The Coy. received orders to cover the valley running from R.14.d.0.0. to LA VACQUERIE, and to pay special attention to the left flank and VILLERS PLOUICH, and also to help the infantry with overhead fire during their advance. O. C. Company reconnoitred the ground and found this was only possible from high ground and at long ranges.

Gun positions were chosen from which section commanders could view the whole action, and thus act according to the situation. These positions were in the open and no infantry were within 100 yards of them.

Exact gun positions were chosen and aiming points laid out on the evening of April 23rd, 1917, by section officers. These positions were dug in the same night, but unfortunately the working party in Q.24 central were stopped for nearly 2 hours by the enemy who put up a heavy barrage, but inflicted no casualties; consequently these emplacements were not well camouflaged as those in R.20d.0.0. which were invisible 50 yards away. This barrage also interfered with intended telephonic communication between guns, which was not available during the battle.

12 guns were available for action, of which 4 were situated in R.20.d.0.0., 6 in Q.24.central and 2 in reserve in sunken road about Q.24.c.2.6.

The action started 4.15.a.m; our artillery barrage was very effective but the enemy replied vigorously. The 17th Welsh Rgt. advanced and obtained their objectives; the battalion on their left also went through VILLERS PLOUICH and obtained their objectives, but for some reason withdrew, thus exposing our flank. On learning this, the two guns in reserve immediately advanced to FIFTEEN RAVINE and were placed at the disposal of O.C. 17th Welsh Regt. The other 10 guns were warned at once of the situation and ordered to keep special vigilance, but no counter-attack took place, and later the battalion of the left advanced to and held their objective.

The lessons learnt from the battle from a machine gunners point of view were many, but especially the following :-

(a) In preparing for an attack aiming posts must be laid out in daylight, as the attack may take place before dawn, and the smoke makes direct laying difficult.

(b) In consequence of the latter it is very hard to engage targets, though in the case of a counter-attack by the enemy, visibility should be better.

(c) Positions dug in the open and cleverly concealed and away from the infantry are safe, and positions dug in without camouflage are very hard to hit.

(d) Close co-operation between battalion commanders and O.C. Coy. is very desirable and necessary, and in this case the infantry commander was confident that his flank was protected by M.G.fire and gave his orders accordingly.

(sd) A.L.Harrison, Major,
Commanding
25/4/17. 119th M.G.Coy.

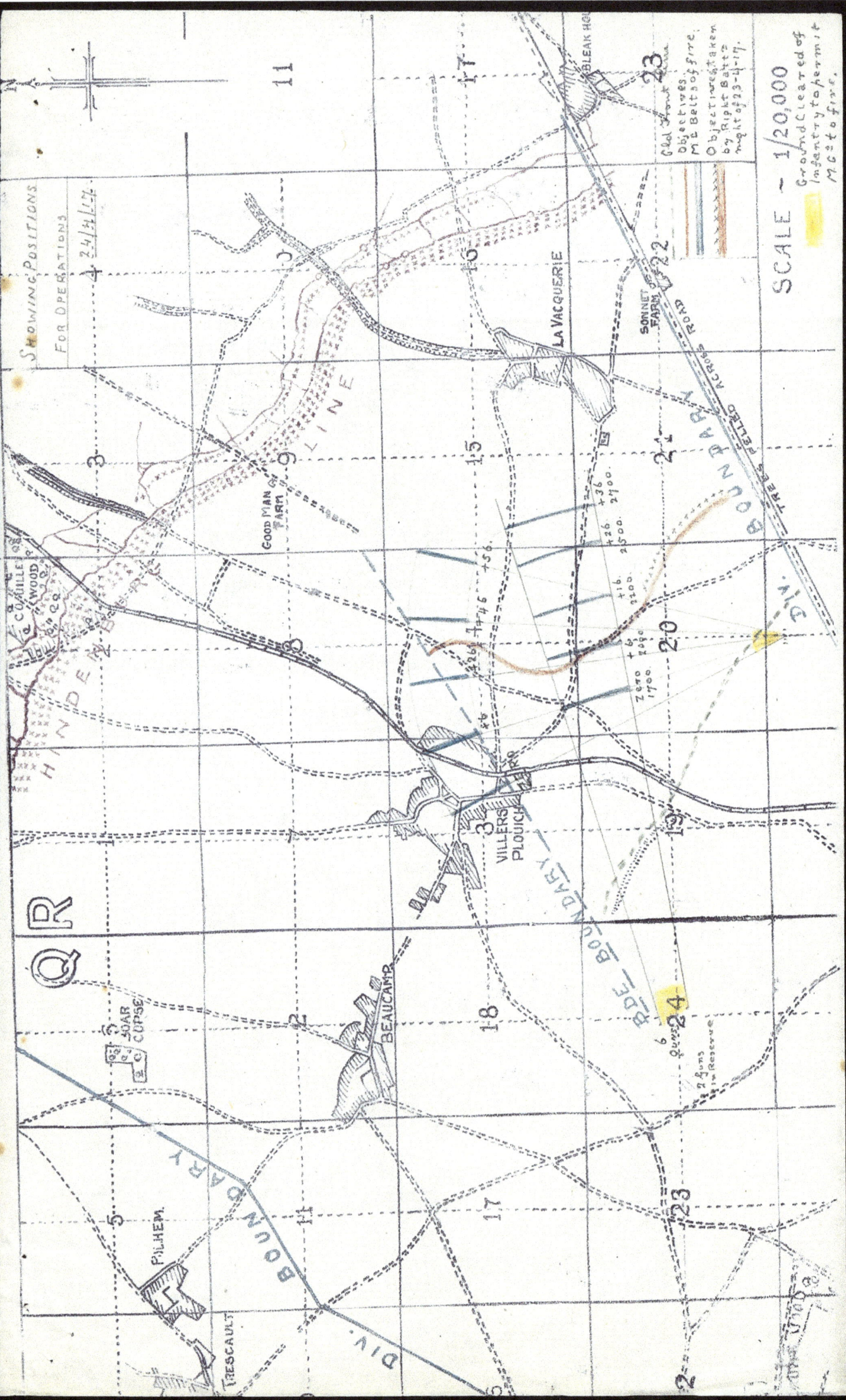

Vol 12

WAR DIARY
of
119th M.G. Coy.

from May 1.17 to May 31.17.

CONFIDENTIAL

WAR DIARY
or
INTELLIGENCE SUMMARY.
(Erase heading not required.)

Army Form C. 2118.

Place	Date	Hour	Summary of Events and Information	Remarks and references to Appendices
GOUZEAUCOURT.	MAY 1ST.		POSITION OF GUNS. 1 at R.20.d.6.4.; 1 at R.26.b.5.5. 4 in FIFTEEN RAVINE R.19.d. 2 doing Anti-Aircraft work in GOUZEAUCOURT. 4 resting at FINS. 4 guns under 2/Lt. LORDEN relieved 4 guns of 120 M.G. Coy in GOUZEAUCOURT WOOD line.	
	2ND.		FRONT LINE. R.14.a.9.b. 8 emplacements dug and camouflaged at R.26.b. central. SUPPORT LINE. FIFTEEN RAVINE. 12 emplacements for operations dug and camouflaged during night at R.26/b central.	
	3RD.	10 a.m.	RELIEF. 4 guns of the 4th Guards M.G. Coy relieved 4 guns of No.1 section in GOUZEAUCOURT WOOD line. After relief No.1 section proceeded to FINS. Coy. H.Q. Bombed by aeroplane. 16 emplacements dug and camouflaged.	
	4TH.		The Coy. co-operated with indirect overhead fire with 119th Infy. Bde. in an extensive raid on LA VACQUERIE. Nos. 1, 2, 3, 4 sections (16 guns) were dug in and camouflaged in position R.26.336 and fired 115,000 rounds. Copy of C.O.'s order attached. (appx?)	
	5TH.		On conclusion of operations no. 2 section relieved no. 3 in FIFTEEN RAVINE, his 1 subsection relieved no. 4 in R.26.b. No.1 subsection proceeded to GOUZEAUCOURT. Nos. 3 & 4 sections proceeded to FINS.	

WAR DIARY or INTELLIGENCE SUMMARY.

Army Form C. 2118.

Place	Date	Hour	Summary of Events and Information	Remarks and references to Appendices
GOUZEAU-COURT IN THE LINE	MAY 6th		GUN POSITIONS. 2 covering FRONT LINE. 2 in Reserve in GOUZEAUCOURT. 2 in FIFTEEN RAVINE. B in FINS.	
	7th		2/Lt VANDYKE F.R. & 2 nt Hertfordshire Regt/M.G.C. joined the Coy. Orders received to prepare by gun Jubilant for the firing of indirect fire positions. Sgt Tew (QUEENS CROSS) No 3 Section obtained from Hospital. 2/Lt H.W. SPURRELL rejoined the Coy from Hospital. C.y H.Q. moved to dug outs in Q29 B 3.0. 2/Lt LORDEN reconnoitred QUARRY R14 A9.0 with 2 guns. Work continued on recover system.	
	8th	MOVE	2/Lt VANDYKE with 2 guns of No 3 Section occupied positions in recover system. Point Q35 C.4.5.	
	9th		Lt EDWARDS T.E. proceeded to FLIXECOURT for course. O.C. reconnoitred the line - very wet.	
	10TH		No 3 & ½ No 4 Sections moved to GOUZEAUCOURT. B Coy H.Q. camouflaged & much improved. Nos. 4 & ½ each of Nos. 1, 2, 3 Sections took up indirect fire positions and put up 15-minute Barrage from 3 p.m. Rounds fired = 13750. Road at Coy H.Q. improved. O.C. Coy visited Bath H.Q. No 4 Section returned to GOUZEAUCOURT at dusk, right half of No 3 Section took up new positions.	
	11TH		Right half of No 1 Section completed emplacements and shelters. O.C. Coy visited guns in front and intermediate lines. Left half relieved right half No 3 Section in front line, No 4 Section relieved No 2 Section in intermediate Line.	
	12TH		O.C. Coy visited the Transport and later reconnoitred the front line.	

Army Form C. 2118.

WAR DIARY
or
INTELLIGENCE SUMMARY.
(Erase heading not required.)

Instructions regarding War Diaries and Intelligence Summaries are contained in F.S. Regs., Part II. and the Staff Manual respectively. Title pages will be prepared in manuscript.

Place	Date	Hour	Summary of Events and Information	Remarks and references to Appendices
IN THE FIELD GOUZEAUCOURT	May 13.		O.C. Coy reconnoitred line. No 2 Section supplied working party at Coy. H.Q. Remaining sections in position, all quiet.	
	14.		No 2 Section relieved No 1 Section in the front line. LIEUT. HERBERT formed 1/2 of No 3 Section if the Brown line. LIEUT. HARKNESS rejoined the Company from U.K.	
	15.		Very heavy rain; many repairs to shelters etc necessary. Indirect fire positions laid out; O.C. Coy reconnoitred the line. No 1 Section refitted at GOUZEAUCOURT	
	16.		Reserve of S.A.A. completed; latrines constructed. Indirect fire control out. O.C. Coy visited the line.	
	17.		1/2 No 3 Section relieved the other 1/2 in the front line. Indirect Fire on selected targets. Observation indifferent. O.C. Coy visited front system and Brown line.	
	18.		Indirect Fire and observation; one German hit, others dispersed. O.C. Coy visited indirect fire positions. No 1 Section relieved gun of No 2, 3, 1 Section. 2 guns of No. 2 relieved 2 guns of No. 4. Lieut HERBERT with 1 gun occupied position on the main road. No 4 Section returned to GOUZEAUCOURT.	
	19.		Indirect fire on selected targets; party of enemy dispersed. LIEUT ANDERTON in O.P. O.C. Coy visited indirect fire positions. At 5 A.M. another brought down, a German balloon forced to descend. Great aerial activity. Indirect Fire on selected targets. LIEUT. ANDERTON in O.P.	
	20.		No 4 Section carried up guns & equipment to new positions. 2/LT. VANDYKE with 2 guns relieved LIEUT. HERBERT in the front line. O.C. Coy visited new indirect Fire positions. No 1 Section constructed emplacement. No 4 Section moved up and occupied new positions under LIEUT. HARKNESS. New position selected in intermediate line and occupied by No 2 section.	
	21.		LIEUT. DEXTER'S 2 guns carried out indirect fire on targets selected. 4 guns of No 1 section and 2 each of No 2, 1 and 2 sections fired barrage from 2.15 a.m. to 2.45 a.m. in accordance with scheme for raid. Rounds fired 27,500. LIEUT. HARKNESS and 4 guns relieved LIEUT. DEXTER in indirect fire positions and intermediate line. O.C. Coy visited transport lines, FINS.	
	22.			

Army Form C. 2118.

WAR DIARY
or
INTELLIGENCE SUMMARY.
(Erase heading not required.)

Instructions regarding War Diaries and Intelligence Summaries are contained in F. S. Regs., Part II. and the Staff Manual respectively. Title pages will be prepared in manuscript.

Place	Date	Hour	Summary of Events and Information	Remarks and references to Appendices
GOUZEAUCOURT	May 23.		Indirect fire on targets continued. 2 machine guns silenced. Several parties of the enemy dispersed. Owing to direct hit the 2 indirect fire guns were moved to new positions.	
	24.		Owing to heavy shelling by LIEUT. DEXTIER and 4 guns moved from GOUZEAUCOURT to W.4.a.1.3.	
			Indirect fire from the new positions commenced. Both sides put up a short barrage during the night. O.C. Coy visited the line and the transport lines at FINS. LIEUT. HERBERT took charge of the transport section vice 2/LT EVANS (proceeding on leave to U.K.)	
	25		1/2 No 3 section in the Brown line relieved 1/2 no 3 in the front line. O.C. Coy visited the line. Indirect fire was continued, a direct hit being obtained on one of the enemy. 2/LIEUT. EVANS proceeded on leave to U.K.	
	26.		Fire was opened by 5 hostile batteries at 8 p.m. without any apparent effect. The enemy shelled the left of the forward area heavily, principally 2 guns of the Coy was relieved on night of 26/27 by parts of 120 & 121st M.G. Coys. Reliefs were as follows:—	
			M.G.1. R.21.c.7510. M.G.2. R.20.a.8085 M.G.3. R.20.a.7090. S. 1. R.26.b.8065. R. 1. R.20.c.4510. R. 2. R.20.c.2520. R. 3. R.19.d.4090. M.G.4. R.14.d.3575. B.1 Q.35c.4040. B.2. Q.35.c.4080. Relieved by 120th M.G. Coy. Relieved by 121st M.G. Coy.	
FINS.	27.		The 2 guns employed for indirect fire were withdrawn on conclusion of relief, the whole company proceeded to billets at FINS. The Coy spent the day cleaning up and improving its billets. Scheme for training was drawn up.	

Army Form C. 2118.

WAR DIARY
or
INTELLIGENCE SUMMARY.
(Erase heading not required.)

Instructions regarding War Diaries and Intelligence Summaries are contained in F. S. Regs., Part II. and the Staff Manual respectively. Title pages will be prepared in manuscript.

Place	Date	Hour	Summary of Events and Information	Remarks and references to Appendices
FINS.	MAY. 28.		Company spent the day as follows:— 2 sections washing limbers, 2 sections training (including Indirect Fire). An elementary class doing elementary work. O.C. Coy visited the BROWN LINE.	
	29.		Training continued as on the previous day. Sports and a concert organised after work.	
	30.		Training for all sections and elementary squads. Competition in immediate Action carried out. Indirect Fire practised.	
	31.		Training continued — lock-stripping + indirect fire by elementary class and sections respectively. New course at the Brigade Bombing School opened.	

A. Mamann
Major

FROM. O.C., 119TH M.G. COY.

TO H.Q. 119TH INFY BDE.

Attached please find War Diary of 119th M.G. Coy. for the month of June, 1917.

IN THE FIELD. H.W. Spurrell 2/Lt for
1-7-17, O.C., 119th M.G. Coy.

119th 7th Machine Gun Coy

WAR DIARY

FOR

JUNE 1917

SECRET

119 M.G.C.

Army Form C. 2118.

WAR DIARY
or
INTELLIGENCE SUMMARY.
(Erase heading not required.)

Place	Date	Hour	Summary of Events and Information	Remarks and references to Appendices
FINS.	JUNE 1.		Training carried out in the morning according to programme. Shoots took place at 2 p.m. These included tests in machine gun work and snapshot work. A concert followed at 7 p.m.	
	2.		LIEUT. VANDYKE proceeded to LONGAVESNES for instruction in co-operation with aircraft. O.C. Coy, LIEUT. ROBINSON, LIEUT. ANDERTON, attended a lecture at H.Q. 119th BDE. Company prepared to take over the line. O.C. Coy, LIEUT. DEXTER & 2/LT DUNN reconnoitred; LIEUT. ANDERTON visited the line to select suitable spots for O.P's.	
			2/LIEUT. LORDEN proceeded to LONGAVESNES for instruction with aircraft.	
VILLERS PLOUICH.	3.		The Company relieved 121st M.G. Coy. in the VILLERS PLOUICH sectors as follows — No 2 Section and 1 gun of No. 3, occupied the front line positions. No. 4 Section occupied intermediate line positions. No. 1 and 3 guns of No. 3 remained in reserve at FINS.	
			O.C. Coy reconnoitred the line twice. Positions were selected for indirect fire. These positions were prepared by No. 1 section which came up from FINS and afterwards returned to Coy H.Q.	
			The enemy put up a heavy barrage during the night for 20 minutes. This slightly injured one machine-gun. Our machine-guns fired 3950 rounds.	
	4.		A quiet day with good observation. No. 1 section finished a shelter at Coy. H.Q. and then proceeded to the indirect fire positions which they completed. 2/LIEUT. LORDEN with 2 guns then occupied the positions.	
			O.C. Coy visited the whole line.	
	5.		O.C. Coy visited the line. No. 2 section was relieved by 2 guns of No. 1 and 1 of No. 3. One extra gun was placed in the front line. Dispositions as follows —	
			No. 3 and 2 guns of No. 1 in front line. 2 guns of No. 1 in indirect fire positions. No. 4 section in intermediate line positions. No. 2 section in reserve.	
			O.C. Coy awarded the D.S.O.	

119 M.G.C.
Army Form C. 2118.

WAR DIARY
or
INTELLIGENCE SUMMARY.
(Erase heading not required.)

Instructions regarding War Diaries and Intelligence Summaries are contained in F. S. Regs., Part II. and the Staff Manual respectively. Title pages will be prepared in manuscript.

Place	Date	Hour	Summary of Events and Information	Remarks and references to Appendices
VILLERS PLOUICH	June 6.		New guns were dug in; 2 being adjusted. Shelters were commenced at 5 P.M. a barrage was put down by both Divnl. Artillery. M.G.'s of Nos 1 & 4 sections co-operated firing on GOOD MAN FARM and PINE COPSE. Rounds expended 10,000. LIEUT. ANDERTON in O.P.	
	7.		O.C. Coy visited the line. Work continued on shelters in the front line and repairs done after heavy fall of rain. Indirect fire continued on targets and directed from O.P. 2 guns of No1 section in I.F. positions relieved 2 guns in front line. O.C. Coy visited FINS and Bde. H.Q.	
	8.	10.15	Our M.G.'s fired indirectly on hostile 77 m.m. battery situated at R.16.A.8 & 5.8. with good effect. LT ANDERTON in O.P. engaged several targets attained observation. D.C.b & c reconnoitred the line during the night.	
	9.		O.C. Coy visited the line. No.2 section relieved No.4 section in the FIFTEEN RAVINE LINE; No.4 section relieved No.3 in the front line; No.3 returned to reserve at Coy H.Q. M.G.'s carried out indirect fire on selected targets; observation was difficult 2/LIEUT. D.M. EVANS returned from leave to U.K.	
	10.		O.C. Coy visited the FIFTEEN RAVINE LINE accompanied by the Corps M.G.O. Indirect fire was carried out with observation. 2/LIEUT. H.W. SPURRELL returned from D/181. R.F.A.	
	11.		O.C. Coy visited the front line. Indirect fire was carried on with observation. Corrections were made for the error of the day.	
	12.		1 gun was moved in the FIFTEEN RAVINE line. O.C. Coy visited the line. 2 guns of No.1 section in indirect fire positions relieved 2 guns in the front line.	
	13.		Indirect fire carried out on GOOD MAN FARM and other targets. No.3 section relieved No.2 in the FIFTEEN RAVINE line. No.2 relieved No.4 in the front line. No.4 returned to Coy H.Q. as section in reserve.	

WAR DIARY
or
INTELLIGENCE SUMMARY.

(Erase heading not required.)

Army Form C. 2118.

119 M.G.C.

Instructions regarding War Diaries and Intelligence Summaries are contained in F. S. Regs., Part II. and the Staff Manual respectively. Title pages will be prepared in manuscript.

Place	Date	Hour	Summary of Events and Information	Remarks and references to Appendices
VILLERS PLOUICH.	June 14.		Indirect fire was carried out on PINE COPSE and other targets with noticeable effect. Our enemy M.G. retaliated by night but did not damage. O.C. Coy visited FIFTEEN RAVINE and later reconnoitred the line.	
	15.		A clear day and much great aerial activity. Indirect fire continued in the evening took the form of counter-Battery work owing to the activity of hostile M.G's. LIEUT. E EDWARDS returned from U.S.A. school FLIXECOURT O.C. Coy visited FIFTEEN RAVINE and M.G. positions and worked on tables of allowances for wind.	
	16.		Indirect fire on hostile machine guns. No. 4 section relieved No. 2 in the front line. O.C. Coy visited the line. LIEUT. HARKNESS proceeded to FINS sick.	
	17.		Indirect fire on selected targets continued. LIEUT. DEXTER proceeded on leave to U.K. N.C.O. in O.P. directed the fire of artillery on to a large German working party. O.C. Coy visited the line and prepared to hand over. S.A. raid by each side took place – neither was successful.	
FINS.	18.		2 guns in FIFTEEN RAVINE were knocked out. The Coy was relieved by 120th M.G.Coy and proceeded to FINS.	
	19.		O.C. Coy proceeded to leave to U.K. The Coy had baths at 8 a.m. No. 2 section relieved 1 section of 120th M.G.Coy. in the BROWN LINE.	
	20.		Training was carried out from 6–7 a.m. and from 8–12 noon. An elementary class was formed. The afternoon was devoted to voluntary games and kit parade. O.C. Coy visited the BROWN LINE.	
	21.		Training continued during the morning. No. 3 section relieved No. 2 in the BROWN LINE. A good concert held in the evening.	
	22.		Training continued in the morning. The afternoon was spent in games.	

119 M.G.C.
Army Form C. 2118.

WAR DIARY
or
INTELLIGENCE SUMMARY.
(Erase heading not required.)

Instructions regarding War Diaries and Intelligence Summaries are contained in F. S. Regs., Part II. and the Staff Manual respectively. Title pages will be prepared in manuscript.

Place	Date	Hour	Summary of Events and Information	Remarks and references to Appendices
IN THE FIELD DESSART WOOD.	June 23.		Training continued in the morning. The elementary class carried out inter-squad competitions. The company practised tactical handling and the German machine.	
	24.		The company moved in the evening to a new site near DESSART WOOD and a new camp was constructed. LIEUTS. ANDERTON & HERBERT returned from AMIENS.	
	25.		Fatigue work in the morning — improvement of camp. LIEUT. ANDERTON relieved LIEUT. VANDYKE in the front line. The rest of the day was free.	
	26.		Company carried out training; also washing limbers. Preliminary heats for Brigade Sports were run off. O.C. Coy. and LIEUTS. HERBERT, EDWARDS, & VANDYKE reconnoitred the line. Lieut. HARKNESS & 2/LT LORDEN reconnoitred the line. Brigade sports took place in the afternoon; the company won 4 first prizes and a second. The Company moved off at 8.45 and relieved 121st M.G. Coy in the GONNELIEU sector, at the close of the relief the distribution of guns was as follows:—	
GONNELIEU.			Front line, 2 guns in SIXTEEN RAVINE under 2/LT. LORDEN. 2 guns on GONNELIEU—LA VACQUERIE road under LIEUT. VANDYKE. 2 guns in front of GONNELIEU CEMETARY under LIEUT. HERBERT. Intermediate line. 4 guns and 1 emergency gun on QUENTIN RIDGE under LIEUT. EDWARDS. 4 guns on CAMBRAI road and FUSILIER RIDGE under LIEUT. HARKNESS & 2/LT. DUNN. Reserve. 1 gun under LIEUT ANDERTON at Coy.H.Q. at W. G. d. 60.05.	
	27.		O.C. Coy. reconnoitred the recent line and SIXTEEN RAVINE guns by day and the other front line guns by night. The day was on the whole quiet; GONNELIEU was heavily shelled in the afternoon.	
	28.		Heavy rain caused much damage to the trenches. O.C. Coy. visited the line. no guns fired during the day.	
	29.		The enemy attempted to raid the front line but were driven off, leaving 2 wounded prisoners behind. Lieut. VANDYKE proceeded to Coy. H.Q. and thence to FINS. O.C. Coy. visited the line.	
	30.		Soon after midnight the enemy shelled the front line; our guns retaliated. No. 2 relieved No. 3 in the front line. No. 1 relieved No. 4 in Reserve line; 2 guns of No. 4 under 2/LT DUNN went to SIXTEEN RAVINE.	F.W. Robinson Lieut a 4.08/119 M.G.C.

A 5834 Wt. W4973 M687 750,000 8/16 D. D. & L. Ltd. Forms/C.2118/13.

WAR DIARY.

110th M.G. Company

July 1917.

Copy No. 1

Army Form C. 2118.

WAR DIARY
or
INTELLIGENCE SUMMARY.
(Erase heading not required.)

119th M.G. Coy   Page 1

Place	Date	Hour	Summary of Events and Information	Remarks and references to Appendices
IN THE FIELD GONNELIEU	July 1st		The enemy put up a heavy barrage on the front line in TWENTY-TWO RAVINE on our right. In the afternoon they bombarded positions N.E. of GOUZEAUCOURT station. Indirect fire was commenced on selected targets but owing to the various observations was difficult.	Ref Map 57cSE. GONNELIEU 1/10000.
	2nd		Major HARRISON and Lieut DEXTER returned from leave to U.K. Lieut. ROBINSON visited the line during the afternoon. Indirect fire continued, Lieut. ANDERTON in O.P. O.C Coy reconnoitred the line. One British and one German aeroplane brought down.	
	3rd		Indirect fire under direction of Lieut. ANDERTON O.P. Heavy bombardment of main CAMBRAI road east of GOUZEAUCOURT station. O.C. visited the line.	
	4th		2/Lt DUNN's 2 guns in SIXTEEN RAVINE relieved by a gun of 120th M.G.Coy. R 8 relieved by another gun of 120th M.S. Coy. Indirect fire continued. O.C. Coy visited the line in the afternoon. Lieut. HARNESS, 2/Lt. DUNN and N°4 section proceeded at sundown to positions on the CAMBRAI road. They co-operated with N°1 section and fired periodically to conceal the noise made in fitting up a Bangalore torpedo in the German wire. After the demonstration the section withdrew to Coy H.Q. Our artillery shelled the enemy heavily in the evening and night.	
	5th		O.C. Coy reconnoitred the line. N°4 Section relieved N°2 in the front line. N°2 section supplied a working party for N°s 1 & 4 to complete emplacements and shelter. N°2 section returned to Coy H.Q.	
	6th		Indirect fire continued; Lieut. ANDERTON in the O.P. O.C. Coy reconnoitred the line and visited Transport lines, FINS.	
	7th		Indirect fire continued on selected targets. Enemy shelled the line N of SIXTEEN RAVINE heavily. Lieut ROBINSON proceeded on leave to U.K.	
	8th		O.C Coy visited the line. Lieuts. EDWARDS & DEXTER reconnoitred with a view to testing out the sniffing guns. The enemy bombarded our front line on the night during the morning; at night petroleum lachrym...	

WAR DIARY
or
INTELLIGENCE SUMMARY.

(Erase heading not required.)

Army Form C. 2118.

Page 11

Place	Date	Hour	Summary of Events and Information	Remarks and references to Appendices
IN THE FIELD GONNELIEU.	JULY 9th		The enemy bombarded the front line heavily during the morning. No. 4 section sustaining 2 casualties. M.G.'s fired on hostile patrols. Indirect fire was carried out on selected targets. No. 2 section relieved No. 3 in the green line; No. 3 relieved No. 1 in the front line; No. 1 returned to Coy. H.Q.	
	10th		O.C. reconnoitred new gun positions in front area. The day was quiet but sounds of a great bombardment could be heard further north.	
	11th		O.C. Coy. went round the line at night and work was commenced on new emplacement and shelter in the gun. Indirect fire was carried out on hostile M.G. positions. Indirect fire was continued. By night an attack of our guns and 2 others fired on S.O.S., going out on the left after a bombardment. The guns also fired to cut a road but as the cordite which was to have blown out the enemy's wire failed to explode, this test was unsuccessful. One of the guns in front was mounted in the new position.	
	12th		O.C. Coy. visited the line twice. No. 4 section relieved No. 2 in the front line; on completion of relief No. 2 relieved No. 1 in the front line and indirect fire positions. No. 1 remained in position during an attempt at raiding which was abandoned as the enemy were lining their own wire. No. 1 then returned to Coy. H.Q. Indirect fire continued through the day.	
	13th		O.C. Coy. visited FINS and reconnoitred the line. Indirect fire carried out on roads and crossroads behind the enemy lines. The enemy's communication trenches were searched as a relief was believed to be in progress.	
	14th		The enemy shelled our communication trench during an infantry relief and forced one of our teams to use the nearest dug-out. A quiet day. Some indirect fire done both day and night. O.C. Coy. fixed new positions in the green line ditch. No. 1 relieved No. 4 in the green line, on quitting the new positions No. 4 relieved No. 3 in	

WAR DIARY
or
INTELLIGENCE SUMMARY.

Army Form C. 2118.

119th M.G. Coy. Page III

Place	Date	Hour	Summary of Events and Information	Remarks and references to Appendices
IN THE FIELD. (SONNELIEU)	July 15		Very heavy rain impeded the work of construction in the green line switch. It was occupied and improvements commenced. 3 concentrations each were carried out on QUARRY TRENCH and SONNET FARM in the evening. O.C. Coy. was present and reconnoitred the line.	
	16		Work on Green line switch continued. Six guns were concentrated on QUARRY TRENCH & SONNET FARM alternately during the early part of the night. Indirect fire covered during the day.	
	17		4 guns concentration on QUARRY TRENCH, SONNET FARM, VILLAGE LANE at dusk. 4 guns concentration on QUARRY TRENCH, SONNET FARM + VILLAGE LANE at dawn.	
	18		O.C. Coy. visited all guns in the line. No 3 Section relieved No 1 Section in the GREEN LINE. No 1 Section then relieved No 4 Section in the FRONT LINE. On completion of relief No 4 Section returned to Coy H.Q.	
	19		O.C. Coy visited all guns in the line during the night.	
	20		LIEUT ROBINSON returned from leave to U.K.	
	21		In answer to a Corps order for a Defence Scheme, drawn up from O.P. No. 1 Section, ... No 3 Section in GREEN LINE No 3 at Coy. a/c No 1 Section the FRONT LINE. No 3 further relieved .... No 2 section. All Coy. HQ.	
	22		Support	
	23		...... Hostile artillery unusual by day. ...... 1 a.m. No Guns concentrated on the unknown ground in front of enemy trenches taken at R.27.6.50,1.5 was at R.26.2540. Fire was maintained for 3 minutes after which a paid of the 17th WELSH REGT. went over and made the ground a forward to our ...... and .... this area - it was hoped that ...... has been ...... Previously in this area - it was hoped that ...... MAJOR HARRISON proceeded to ENGLAND to join the MACHINE GUN TRAINING CENTRE GRANTHAM. LIEUT D.J. EMERY. RA ...... "Second in command" of the Coy.	

WAR DIARY or INTELLIGENCE SUMMARY

Army Form C. 2118.

Page IV

Place	Date	Hour	Summary of Events and Information	Remarks and references to Appendices
IN THE FIELD. GONNELIEU.	July 25.		Orders arrived for Lt E.G. HERBERT to proceed to 121 Machine Gun Company as 2nd in command vice Lt D.J. AMERY-PARKES. Night firing was carried out on the following lengths R22.c.4.3. R22.b. R22.b. SONNET FARM and QUARRY TRENCH. Enemy quiet.	
	July 26		At 6 a.m. this morning the enemy opened a heavy bombardment all along the right Bde front and on battery positions around GAUCHE WOOD and VILLERS GUISLAIN. The bombardment ceased at 7.30 a.m. The C.O. visited all the guns in the line. The following night took place No.1 Lieut Jan relieves No.3. No.3 relieves No.4. No.4 relieves No.2 which relieves to lay H.Q. Night firing was carried out on the following lengths – R.20 central, SONNET FARM, QUARRY & BARRIER TRENCHES R38.d.80.35 to R22.9.90.50. R22.c.18.10 - R22.c.40.15. - 3750 rnds.	
	July 27th	2/45	D.M. EVANS was gazetted Lieutenant to date from July 1st 1917. Night firing was carried out on the following lengths. Searchlight at BLEAK HOUSE. R.15.c.00.66. R23.c.5.9. R14.c.15.56. R22.c.25.31. T road R22.a.90.15. QUARRY TRENCH & BARRIER TRENCH. 7250 rounds fired.	
	July 28		The normal return went to HEUDICOURT for baths this morning. Night firing was carried out on QUARRY TRENCH at 12 midnight a Bn 6 gun barrage was put	

WAR DIARY
or
INTELLIGENCE SUMMARY.
(Erase heading not required.)

Army Form C. 2118.

Page V

Place	Date	Hour	Summary of Events and Information	Remarks and references to Appendices
	July 28		on to BLEAR TRENCH - no observation of reculili was obtained.	
	July 29		O.C. went round the line. Lt VANDYCK regained the Company from CAMIERS. The usual night firing took place on QUARRY TRENCH, LA VACQUERIE and VILLAGE LANE.	
	July 30		O.C. by visits all guns in the line. The machine gun Barrage for the following operation was arranged. Relief took place No.2 section relieving No.1 Lewis No.1 section " No.3 " returned to H.Q. The usual night firing took place.	
	July 31		O.C. Company reconnoitres positions for the barrage. A very wet day. Usual night firing on CAMBRAI RD. BONNET FM. BLEAK HOUSE.	

APPENDIX I
Army Form C. 2118.

WAR DIARY
or
INTELLIGENCE SUMMARY
(Erase heading not required.)

STATEMENT OF STRENGTH, ETC.

STRENGTH OF COMPANY   July 1st — 12 Off. 175 O.R.
"   "   July 31st — 11 Off. 175 O.R.

DETAILS.

STRENGTH INCREASE.
    Lt D.J. AMERY-PARKES.
    Nil O.R.

STRENGTH DECREASE.
    MAJOR A.L. HARRISON. D.S.O. (to Openshaw)
    LT E.G. HERBERT.   (to 121 M.G. Coy)
    Nil O.R.

COURSES.   Lt VANDYCKE & 10 O.R. CARRIERS.

ROUNDS FIRED   142,000 rounds.

Army Form C. 2118.

Copy No. 1

WAR DIARY
or
INTELLIGENCE SUMMARY.
(Erase heading not required.)

Vol 15

WAR DIARY.

119 M. G. Company.

From August 1st 1917   To Aug 31st 1917.

WAR DIARY or INTELLIGENCE SUMMARY

Army Form C. 2118.

Page 1

Place	Date	Hour	Summary of Events and Information	Remarks and references to Appendices
GONNELIEU	1st August		O.C. Coy went round the line. All preparations were completed for the raid. Weather wet and windy. At 1 am the bombardment for the raid commenced. 8 Stokes Mortars attacked and put down on RA50 and RI50 for 10 minutes. 4 guns of No 1 Section BLEAR SUPPORT and Gunman lines in RI5C to accumulate this barrage. At 1:10 am an intense bombardment was put down on BARRIER TRENCH and neighbouring trenches. Guns of Nos 2, 3 & 4 Sections cooperating with a barrage on BLEAR TRENCH, BLEAR WALK, BARRIER TRENCH and VILLAGE LANE. At 1:13 am the infantry entered the German front line trench through a gap previously blown by bangalore torpedoes. At 1:40 am the infantry withdrew. At 4 am the barrage ceased and guns returned to their battle emplacements. Number of rounds fired was 60000. No prisoners were taken in the raid. O.C. Company visited 180 M.G. Coy to arrange relief. Weather very wet.	Reference Map 1/10000 BONNELIEU 57cSE. For areas & Maps of this raid see Appendix!!

WAR DIARY or INTELLIGENCE SUMMARY

Army Form C. 2118.

Page II

Place	Date	Hour	Summary of Events and Information	Remarks and references to Appendices
GONNELIEU	3rd August		The following reliefs took place last night owing to the Division Reverting to entire "B" front North. No 2 Sec was relieved by a section of 121 M.G. Coy. No 1 Section changed places with a section of 144 M.G. Coy in the GREEN LINE. No 3 Section relieved a section of 120 M.G. Coy in the VILLERS PLOUICH Sector. The result of these reliefs was that the Company sis a side slip to the left. Coy H.Q. remained in its present position. Night firing was carried out on SONNET FARM, VILLAGE LANE and KAVACQUERIE. Weather wet.	
	4th August		Last night after the relief the enemy attempted to raid our trenches in R.14.d. but was repulsed leaving 7 rifles 500 rounds and an advance scouting station behind him. O.C. Company visited the main positions on the eye. No 2 Section relieves No 1 Section on the GREEN LINE. No 1 Section returning	

Army Form C. 2118.

WAR DIARY
or
INTELLIGENCE SUMMARY.
(Erase heading not required.)

Page ___

Instructions regarding War Diaries and Intelligence Summaries are contained in F. S. Regs., Part II. and the Staff Manual respectively. Title pages will be prepared in manuscript.

Place	Date	Hour	Summary of Events and Information	Remarks and references to Appendices
GONNEHEM	4th		To Bn H.Q. O.C. Coy reconnoitred the line with a view to putting two more guns in on the left. Weather wet all day.	
	5th		The usual night firing took place. Weather wet all day. O.C. Coy visited the Transport lines in the afternoon. Orders came for Lt. F.W. Robinson to take over command of the 23rd Machine Gun Company. Lt. Edwards Assumed command over the duties of second in command as usual. Night firing was carried out as usual.	
	6th		Lt. F.W. Robinson left the Company to join the 23rd M.G. Company and was struck off the strength. O.C. Coy visited all guns on the line. Two new guns No. 7 and 8 were put in on the left of WELSH TRENCH. The usual night firing was carried out.	
	7th		O.C. Company visited the line. The weather was very wet. The usual night firing was carried out.	

A5834 Wt.W4973/M687 750,000 8/16 D.D. & L. Ltd. Forms/C.2118/13

Army Form C. 2118.

WAR DIARY
or
INTELLIGENCE SUMMARY.
(Erase heading not required.)

Page IV

Place	Date	Hour	Summary of Events and Information	Remarks and references to Appendices
GONNELIEU	August 8th		The following relief took place last night, ½ No 1 Section relieved ½ No 2 Section. No 3 Section relieved No 2 Section (i.e. to GREEN LINE) ½ No 2 Section relieved ½ No 4 Section. The two I.F. guns were withdrawn & No 4 Section returned to Company H.Q. Weather very wet. No night firing was carried out owing to the relief.	
	August 9th		O.C. Coy went round the line with O.C. Sussex al Machine Gun Company who are shortly to relieve us. O.C. Coy was round the Acting rank of Captain. Weather very wet in the afternoon. Night firing was carried out on LA VACQUERIE, CORNER SUPPORT and R16. This afternoon 1st ANDERTON manned Mr. G. & gun and opened fire on a large party of Germans. Several were seen to drop, the remainder running as fast as they could to a trenches road.	
	August 10		The Sgt Major was wounded this evening by a Machine Gun bullet in the hand. Night firing was carried on LA VACQUERIE VILLAGE NAME &c.	

Army Form C. 2118.

WAR DIARY
or
INTELLIGENCE SUMMARY.
(Erase heading not required.)

Instructions regarding War Diaries and Intelligence Summaries are contained in F. S. Regs., Part II. and the Staff Manual respectively. Title pages will be prepared in manuscript.

Place	Date	Hour	Summary of Events and Information	Remarks and references to Appendices
GONNELIEU	August 11th		O.C. Company visited the line. One gun fired by day on CORNER SUPPORT & neighbouring trenches with a view to putting down German sniper shooting. Reports received from the Infantry that some considerable effect as snipers were much quieter in the afternoon and evening. The usual night firing was carried out on VILLAGE LANE & CORNER TR. all weather very wet.	
	12th		Crews went receivers for the rain tonight. Operation orders were issued and all preparations made. A telephone line was run from the left gun of 6 guns to Left Battalion Headquarters. O.C. Company visited the line. 1st Guns were in position by 12 midnight. There were bursts into two groups of 6 guns each. The left group under Lt ANDERTON the right group under Lt EDWARDS. The left group were in NEWPORT TRENCH about R.14.d.7.6. and were firing on a barrage line from R.21.c.9090 to R.22.c.50.80. The right group fired up into 3 subsections situated about R.26.c.4040. and fired on @ CAMBRAI ROAD from SONNET FARM to	

WAR DIARY
or
INTELLIGENCE SUMMARY.
(Erase heading not required.)

Army Form C. 2118.

Page VI

Place	Date	Hour	Summary of Events and Information	Remarks and references to Appendices
GONNELIEU	12th cont	R22c 6045.	(c) SONNET TRENCH (c) BARRACK TRENCH from R22c 2050 to	
	13th	R22c 4500.	O.C. Coy went to ascertain Bn HQ at 12:45 the tobacco was not in position so it was decided to fullpone the raid. Hay an hour. This was only first communicated to the guns in time to it to 130 am. At 1:20 am the Tobacco was still not prevent them from firing. At 1:20 am the Tobacco was still not in position so it was decided to first cancel the raid. The code BBB was sent through to all guns and they returned to their battle positions. The following lessons were learnt.	

(1) The necessity of a separate telephonic communication for the Machine guns as the line at coy Bn HQ was so congested by the artillery and Infantry that O.C. Coy was only able to get through to O.C. Byll coy 1 minute before zero.

(2) The necessity of a separate numum communication as the numum has to be to stop the night coup during the congestion on

Army Form C. 2118.

Page VII

WAR DIARY
or
INTELLIGENCE SUMMARY.
(Erase heading not required.)

Place	Date	Hour	Summary of Events and Information	Remarks and references to Appendices
GONNELIEU	13th		the Wiltshires. (3) The necessity to meet all eventualities is full foremost. Cease fire, continue fire. Weather was very wet all morning and afternoon but cleared up considerably in the evening. Orders were issued for the relief of the Company tonight by the Divisional Machine Gun Company. The relief started at 10 pm and was completed by 1 am which was quick considering the status of the ground and the fact that all full teams had to be brought up. On relief the Company returned to billets occupied vacated by 15/144 Company at HEUDICOURT.	
HEUDICOURT	14th		The day was spent in cleaning up and overhauling all gun equipment. Weather was very wet.	
	15th		Programme of training was commenced. A copy of this is attached. O.C. Company includes the usual full general work and training.	See Appendix III

A5834 Wt W4973/M687 750,000 8/16 D. D. & L. Ltd. Forms/C.2118/13

Army Form C. 2118.

WAR DIARY
or
INTELLIGENCE SUMMARY.
(Erase heading not required.)

Page VIII

Place	Date	Hour	Summary of Events and Information	Remarks and references to Appendices
HEUDICOURT	August 16th		Programme of training was continued. Weather very bad. The Company fired the 244 M.G. Company Transport at Soccer.	Map Reference 57 c S.E. 20000.
	August 17th		Programme of training was continued. S.C. employed a ordinary gun course at the Divisional Gas School at FINS. The Staff Captain inspected the billets this morning. Weather fine.	
	August 18th		Programme of training continued. Orders were received that this company would have to provide 13 guns to assist the 121 M.G. Coy in a Machine Gun Barrage for an operation to be carried out by the 12th Suffolk Regt on the 21st inst at 4.15 a.m. Weather fine.	
	August 19th		Church Parade at 11 a.m. Orders were received that the operation for night 21/22 has been postponed until the 22/23. Weather very fine.	
	August 20th		Programme of training continued. O.C. Company visited O.C. 121 M.G. Company and arranged details for the forthcoming operations. Weather very fine.	

Army Form C. 2118.

WAR DIARY or INTELLIGENCE SUMMARY.

(Erase heading not required.)

Page IX

Place	Date	Hour	Summary of Events and Information	Remarks and references to Appendices
HEUDICOURT	Aug 2/17		Programme of training continued. Company Operation Orders for tomorrow were issued. A copy is attached as Appendix IV. Guns of No 1, 3 & 4 Batteries with No 1, 2 & 3 of same under Lts ANDERTON, DEXTER and SPURRELL went up at dusk time to trenches and built their gun positions for the operations. It was thought that the enemy might attempt to make a raid on our lines so guns were ordered to maintain in their battery positions and be ready to open fire on Enemy Front line. Nothing unusual occurred during the night.	Reference Map 57cS.E. 1/20,000 See Appendix IV
		3:30 am	Guns remained at Stand To and were taken to trenches and dugouts near the Battle positions for the day. In the afternoon orders were received that the operation was cancelled and that our guns had to remain in position until dusk on the 3rd and fire concentrations at the following times — 10 pm 11:30 pm and	
		12:15 am	They were also to be ready to open fire should the enemy attempt to make a raid	

A 5834. Wt.W4973/M687. 750,000. 8/16. D. D. & L. Ltd. Forms/C.2118/13.

Army Form C. 2118.

WAR DIARY
or
INTELLIGENCE SUMMARY.
(Erase heading not required.)

Place	Date	Hour	Summary of Events and Information	Remarks and references to Appendices
HEUDICOURT	23rd		Last night our twelve guns fire concentrations at the previously stated times are bell. Mg gun at each orientation. Otherwise the night was very quiet. Rounds fine & good. The guns were with drew at dusk and proceeded back to billets independently. Weather fine a little rain during the night.	Map 57cSE. Corps
	24th		The first line have were spent in cleaning up generally. The last hour Infantry Company Bull was attempted for the first time since the Company came out and was very successful. 3's Bull has now been established in the Company and all movements are in line. Routine to take place in 4's. Q Company parade was held at the Y.M.C.A. at 6 pm and was a great success.	
	25th		Programme of training continued. Men returned from leave. It have proceeded on leave. Weather fair. To United Kingdom.	

Army Form C. 2118.

WAR DIARY
or
INTELLIGENCE SUMMARY.
(Erase heading not required.)

Page X1

Place	Date	Hour	Summary of Events and Information	Remarks and references to Appendices
HEUDICOURT	Aug 26th		The usual Church Parades were attended in the morning. Weather very wet all day.	Weather See WWWD
	27th		Programme of training continues. The Staff Captain inspected the billets this afternoon. Weather very windy.	
	28th		All gun pits etc were cleaned this morning prior to going into the line again. Orders were received that the Company would relieve the 244 M.G. Coy in our old sector on the night 29/30th. The Company Scouts Ld to the afternoon and the final of the interrior competition. No 2 & 4 leads up. The Company has better than this morning (seems to be ready for the line.) O.C. Company visited O.C. 244 Company and arranged all details of relief. Lt & Lieutenants moved off and mounted the guns as follows :-	
			No 1 Section R. 1, 2, 3 & 4 Green Line. No 2 Section Reserve No 3 Section M.G. 1, 2, 3, & 4 No 4 Section M.G. 5, 6, 7, & 8.	

Army Form C. 2118.

Page XII

WAR DIARY
or
INTELLIGENCE SUMMARY.
(Erase heading not required.)

Place	Date	Hour	Summary of Events and Information	Remarks and references to Appendices
CONNEKIEU	Aug 30th		Relief was complete by 12.15 am. OC, 2/y visited OC. 1st Welch Regt. and arranged details for the raid tonight, also the left 6 guns and issued operation orders for tonight. Guns were in position to there concerned. A copy is attached as Appendix. The 6 guns were in position and ready to fire by 9.30 pm. Weather was wet for the first part of the night. L/Cpl Wright was killed by a sniper when the shell hole from. Nothing happened during the night and guns returned to their	Ref. map 57c SE 1/20,000 Refer to Appendix V
	Aug 31st		battle position without incident having fired visited the guns, both Battalions and Brigade. OC company opposite our HQ R21c 8060 at 2.30 pm. Wright was busy their last night's operations would be rehearsed with orders were issued that Machine guns would open fire slowly on their difference line as soon as they came up into position. Guns were in position by 10 pm and commenced firing slowly, weather cloudy, wet all day but fine night.	

A.5834 Wt.W4973/M687 750,000 8/16 D. D. & L. Ltd. Forms/C.2118/13

Army Form C. 2118.

WAR DIARY
or
INTELLIGENCE SUMMARY.
(Erase heading not required.)

Place	Date	Hour	Summary of Events and Information	Remarks and references to Appendices
GONNEHEM			**Minutes for August** Strength of Company August 1st. 11 off 175 O.R. " " " August 31st. 10 " 181 O.R. Strength Decrease. Lt F.W. Robinson. (for wings.) 1 O.R. killed 3 O.R. Strength Increase 9 O.R. on the 22nd Sgt Hunnaball 19th Changes. Lt P.W. Dexter. Carriers. 4 O.R. " Sgt Penington M.G. cone GRANTHAM Rounds fired during the month. — 137000. RDS.	

Lt F.W. Robinson appointed to command 23rd M.G. Coy.

War Plans
Offensive

Appendix III Copy No 1.

Operation Orders
119th Machine Gun Coy.

July 31st 1917

Map. 57c S.E. 1/20000.

① On the night of 1st/2nd August 1917 the 12th S.W.B. will raid the enemy's front line in R.22.c.

② The 119th M.G. Coy. will put up a 16 gun barrage to assist the operation.

③ Dispositions

No 1 Section will take up four positions about R1 + R2. GREEN LINE and will fire on BARRACK TRENCH from R28 a 08.10. to R28 a 12.26. (2 guns) and road in R22 c 95.20 to R22 d 10.40 (2 guns)

No 2 Section will take up positions about R26 b 37.53. and fire on BLEAK TRENCH from R28 c 28.90 to R28 d 10.55.

No 3 Section will take up positions about R26 b 40.27 and will fire on BLEAK WALK (2 guns) and on BARRIER TRENCH from R26 b 95.48 to R.22 b 10.90.

No 4 Section will take up four positions about R26 b 50.80 and will fire on VILLAGE

(3) Cont.
   LANE to the CAMBRAI ROAD a1R.22b.15.30.

(4) All guns will be in position by 12-30 AM.
    2nd August 1917.

(5) 4 pack mules will report to O.C. No 2 Section
    at 9-30 P.M. to convey his guns from the
    front line. These pack mules will return
    to the LARGE QUARRY. O.C. No 2 Section
    making his own arrangements for them
    to convey his guns back.

(6) Zero time and times of firing will be
    notified later.

(7) O.C. Sections will see that there are
    5 boxes of S.A.A. at each gun position.

(8) Position of Coy. H.Q. will be notified later.

(9) Watches will be synchronised at left
    Batt. H.Q. at 6 P.M. 1st August.

(10) Acknowledge.

Operation Orders. Cont.
119th M.G. Coy.   SECRET

① Zero hour will be 1.0 a.m.

② O.C. Coy will be at Left Batt. H.Q. after 12 midnight.

③ Communication between O.C. Coy and Section officers will be by runner. There will be 1 runner per section at Left Batt. Headquarters (these will be provided from the runners at Coy H.Q.) and 1 runner per section with the guns.

④ Section Officers will report by runner to O.C. Coy when all guns are in position.

⑤ No. 1 Section's barrage is cancelled and they will place a barrage on BLEAK SUPPORT R.28.b.00.25 to R.25.a.44.3 (approx) (to conform with the Chinese attack), from ZERO to ZERO plus 10 minutes and then to cease fire.

⑥ The two indirect fire guns will, in addition to their ordinary barrage place a barrage on GERMAN FRONT LINE in R15a. from ZERO to ZERO +10.

(7) At ZERO +10 Nos 2.3+4 sections will fire on the barrage lines already given them and continue firing until ZERO + 60 (subject to further orders).

At ZERO + 60 minutes all guns will cease fire unless 2 white Very lights are fired in the shape of a V. This will be the signal for the barrage to continue until further orders from O.C. Coy.

(8) The rate of fire will not exceed the rate of belt filling.

(9) Great care must be taken with tripod legs and guns must be frequently checked by clinometer.
Night firing boxes will be used.

(10) In the event of unforeseen circumstances causing raid not to be carried out the code B.B.B will be wired to C.X. advanced upon receipt of which all guns will immediately return to their battle positions.

(11) Acknowledge.
1-8-17

DH Clemens actg Capt
OC 119th M.G. Coy

Appendix IV.   Copy 1

Operation Order. No 3
By Capt D. J Amery-Parkes Comd 119th M.G. Coy
Ref map. 57cSE Special sheet 1/10,000

① General Scheme.
The 12th Batt Suffolk Reg. are raiding the enemy trenches about R.28.c. on the night August 22/23rd.

② Machine Guns.
The 119th M.G. Coy. will provide 12 guns to assist in a machine gun barrage to cover the operation.

③ Disposition.
No 1 Section will fire from about R.26.b.10.20 on to Trench from R.28.a.5020 to R.28.a.7070
No 3 Section will fire from R.26.b.0050 on to Trench from R.28.a.20.30 to R.22.c.5010
No 4 Section will fire from R.32.a.5090 on to Trench from R.28.a.20.30 to R.29.c.20.35.

④ Move Equipment & S.A.A. etc.
Guns of Nos 1, 3, & 4 sections will move up to their positions on the night 21/22nd August and will remain for the night in trenches and billets near the gun positions
Nos 1, 2 & 3 will accompany each gun.
Lts Anderton and Dexter will supervise this
On the afternoon of August 22nd the remaining officers and gun numbers will join their sections. Officers will then lay out their zero lines etc

⑤ S.A.A.
13 full belt boxes will be taken up with each gun and 3 boxes of S.A.A.

(6) All guns are to be in position and ready to fire by 9.30 p.m.
(7) Water, oil, etc will be taken up with the guns.
(8) <u>Report</u> when guns are laid and during the operation to Coy H.Q. at
(9) <u>Communication</u>
2 Orderlies will be with each group and 1 for each group at Coy H.Q. Urgent messages by wire from nearest Infty. Coy H.Q.
(10) <u>Synchronisation</u>
Watches will be synchronised at Left Batt H.Q. Right Bde. at 8 P.M.
(11) <u>Special signal</u>
Should it be impossible for the raid to take place, 2 white very lights will be fired from R.27.a.1.3 as a signal for the M.G's not to fire.
(12) Screens will be used to screen the flashes.
(13) Guns will be frequently checked by clinometer. Night firing boxes will be used.
(14) <u>Rates and times of fire</u> will be as follows.

Zero to Zero + 2   2 mins.
Zero + 20 to Zero + 22 2 mins
Zero + 2 hrs 55 mins to Zero + 3 hrs 45 mins   45 mins

Rate of fire 100 rds per gun per minute.

(15) <u>Zero hour</u> will be 10 P.M.
(16) <u>Transport.</u> Section Officers will make their own arrangements re transport for and during the operation.
(17) After the operation sections will return to billets independently.
(18) <u>Medical Arrangements.</u>

Adv Dressing Station   R27 d 04
Aid Post   R26 d 70.05
Dressing Station   X 3 d 0010

(19) <u>Gas.</u> Every precaution to be taken against hostile gas shells.
(20) Acknowledge.

Issue 1 Copies   1,2 & 3   War Diary   O.C. 119th M.G. Coy.
                 4,5,6 & 7 Section Commanders
                 8   O.C.
                 9   O.C. 120th M.G. Coy
                 10   D.M.G.O.
                 11   File

Appendice

TRAINING ORDERS BY CAPT. H.T. AMERY PATTERSON
COMMANDING N°4 M.G. COY.

DAY	7.30 – 8	9 – 10	10 – 11	11.15 – 12.30	AFTERNOON	NIGHT
1st DAY	P.T.	GUN DRILL	ARMS DRILL	STOPPAGES	RECREATIONAL TRAINING	
2nd DAY	P.T.	BOX RESPIRATOR DRILL	REVOLVER SHOOTING GUN DRILL	MECHANISM		NIGHT FIRING 2 SECTIONS
3rd DAY	P.T.	ADVANCED GUN DRILL	ARMS DRILL REVOLVER SHOOTING	BELT FILLING		NIGHT FIRING 2 SECTIONS
4th "	P.T.	RANGE 2 SECTIONS	PACK ANIMAL DRILL	STOPPAGES		
5th "	P.T.	RANGE 2 SECTIONS	PACK ANIMAL DRILL	STOPPAGES		
6th "	R.T.					
7th "	P.T.	ARMS DRILL REVOLVER SHOOTING	ACTION FROM LIMBERS N°S 1 & 2 Secs	USE OF COVER		NIGHT FIRING 2 SECTIONS
8th "	P.T.	BOX RESPIRATOR DRILL	GUN DRILL			NIGHT FIRING 2 SECTIONS
9th "	R.T.	MACHINE GUNS IN ATTACK				
10th "	P.T.	MACHINE GUNS IN DEFENCE				

Issued by Capt D.T. Amery-Parkes 2nd

Appendix V

DAY	7:30-8	9-10	10-11	11:15-12:30	AFTERNOON	NIGHT
11th DAY	P.T.	GUN DRILL	BOX RESPIRATOR DRILL	T.D.	RECREATIONAL TRAINING	
12th	P.T.	ARMS DRILL / REVOLVER SHOOTING	PACKING LIMBERS	PASSING ORDERS		
13th	P.T.	COMPANY SPORTS				

Elementary Class separate until all tests have been passed.

D.T. Amery-Parkes Capt
O.C. 119 Coy

Lichfield

Operation Orders No. 4. Appendix VI
By Capt. D. J. AMERY-PARKES
Commanding 119th M.G. Coy.

1. To-night (30/31-8-17) the 17th WELSH REGt are raiding enemy lines from R15a 85.95 to R9c 10.13.

2. 119th M.G. Coy will co-operate with a barrage.

3. Disposition as follows:-
   No. 4 Section. in position about FRIMLEY TRENCH will fire on trench from R15a 93.85 to R9d 22.95.
   No. 1 Section will fire from neighbourhood of I.F. position on M.G at R15c.55.60 (2 guns) and on CORNER TRENCH from R15a 73.30 to R15a 80.70 (2 guns).

4. To assist No. 4 Section, No. 2 Section will send up two guns complete with belt boxes to report to O.C. No. 4 Section as soon as possible after dark.

5. ZERO time will be the time at which the Bangalore explodes. Should Section Officer not hear the Bangalore they will take the time from artillery.

6. Guns will fire from ZERO to ZERO + 20' in short sharp bursts.

7. ZERO + 20' to ZERO + 60' guns will "stand by" if fire is to be continued the "Code word" REPEAT with the number of minutes after it.
At ZERO + 60' or at end of the "REPEAT" guns will pack up and return to Battle position.

8. Should it be impossible for the raid to take place, the code word "BITCHED" will be sent through, on receipt of which guns will return to Battle position.

9. Under any circumstances guns will be withdrawn at 3.30 A.M. 31-8-17.

10. Section Officers will arrange to have Orderlies at the nearest telephone.

11. Transport has been arranged.

12. Acknowledge.

30-8-17.   O.C. 119 M.G. Coy.

Army Form C. 2118.

WAR DIARY
or
INTELLIGENCE SUMMARY.
(Erase heading not required.)

Instructions regarding War Diaries and Intelligence Summaries are contained in F. S. Regs., Part II. and the Staff Manual respectively. Title pages will be prepared in manuscript.

Place	Date	Hour	Summary of Events and Information	Remarks and references to Appendices

A 5834. Wt. W 4973/M687 750,000 8/16 D. D. & L. Ltd. Forms/C.2118/13

Copy I

Army Form C. 2118.

WAR DIARY
or
INTELLIGENCE SUMMARY.
(Erase heading not required.)

Copy. 1

8/6/16

WAR DIARY.

119 Machine Gun Company

From September 1st 1917 To September 30th 1917.

WAR DIARY
or
INTELLIGENCE SUMMARY
(Erase heading not required.)

Army Form C. 2118.

B Page 1.

Place	Date	Hour	Summary of Events and Information	Remarks and references to Appendices
GONNELIEU	Sept 1st		The ? guns for the raid give intermittent rear fire team through from the O.C. 17th Welsh Regt. Guns were both in their battle positions by 2 am. The raid did not take place owing to the missing Party meeting a Boche party outside his wire. O.C Company visited the guns. Work was started on the New Company H.Q. at GOUZEAUCOURT STATION R.31.a.90.90. The following concentrations were fired each night. 9 - 9.10 9.30 - 9.40 } Trench Tramway 10.15 - 10.25 } R.15.a.83.75. R.15.a.86.97. 10.30 - 10.35 } R.15.a.95.60. R.15.a.70.50. Rounds fired 10000. Orders were issued for an intersection relief which lasts place after dusk. No 1 section relieves No 3 section who came back to H.Q. No 1 and No 4 sections change places. Relief was complete by 10.15 pm. No night firing with Plan - Weather nothing.	Map 57cSE 1/10000 1130 - 1140 } Trench Tramway 1150 - 11.55 } R.15.c.73.55.

Army Form C. 2118.

WAR DIARY
or
INTELLIGENCE SUMMARY.
(Erase heading not required.)

Page II

Place	Date	Hour	Summary of Events and Information	Remarks and references to Appendices
BONNELIEU	2/9/3		O.C. Company visited the line and both battalions. Wealther fine. Alm't 4 pm a German aeroplane came over by our centre section H.Q. and dropped letters and leaflets. One of these was picked up and sent to Brigade H.Q.	Map 57c S.E. 20000.
	4		The following concentrations were fired last night:— 9.15 – 9.25) 9.40 – 9.50) New Work 10.10 – 10.15) R.22 & 30.40 9.30 – 9.40) Trench Tramway 10.15 – 10.20) R.15.0.70.80. 11 – 11.15) 11.20 – 11.30 Concentration F. O.C. Company visited the line and both battalions. Pte Brunts No 4 section was wounded by a bullet in the neck at about 1130 this morning. Weather very fine.	
	5		The following concentrations were fired last night. 9 – 9.15) 9.45 – 9.55) Concentration A. 10.40 – 10.50) 11.30 – 11.45) 9.20 – 9.30) Machine gun at 10.15 – 10.20) R.15.b.5.5. 11.10 – 11.15)	

Army Form C. 2118.

WAR DIARY
or
INTELLIGENCE SUMMARY.
(Erase heading not required.)

Page III

Place	Date	Hour	Summary of Events and Information	Remarks and references to Appendices
CONNERIEU	6th		The following concentrations were fired during the night.	
		9 - 9.10	} Trench Tramway R.15.0.70.25.	
		9.15 - 9.30		
		9.40 - 10.		
		10.5 - 10.20		
		10.30 - 10.40	} Trench R.22.a.50.25.	
		12.30 - 12.40		
			O.C. Company visited the line. Day firing was carried out from the I.F. Pavilions on 15 CORNER TRS R.15.c. and d. Owing to last nights storm the ground was too wet to observe the strike of the bullets.	
			The new improved light F.O. mountings were tested on the range but failed to show sufficient improvement on the old one to warrant it being adopted as a general pattern.	
			Weather fine except for some rain in the evening. MWB	
			The following reliefs took place last night.	
			No 3 section relieves No 1 section in H.Q.	
			No 4 section relieves No 2 section.	

7th

Army Form C. 2118.

Page IV

WAR DIARY
or
INTELLIGENCE SUMMARY.
(Erase heading not required.)

Place	Date	Hour	Summary of Events and Information	Remarks and references to Appendices
BONNELIEU	7th		O.C. Company visited the line and both battalions. Enemy Artillery more lively than usual in the afternoon. Weather very fine.	Map 57.S.E. 1/20000
	8th		The following concentrations were fired last night.	
		8.45 - 9 pm		
		9.10 - 9.20 "	Concentration B	10 - 10.10 pm — New Trench
		9.30 - 9.40 "		10.30 - 10.45 pm — R.16.a.80.35
				11.15 - 11.30 " — to
				11.40 - 11.50 " — R.16.b.10.80
			O.C. Company visited the line in the morning. Weather foggy	
	2/15		O.C. Tunnel Shafts on leave to the U.K.	
			The following concentrations were carried out last night.	
		8.50 - 9 pm		10.20 - 10.25 pm
		9.10 - 9.15 "		10.30 - 10.45 "
		9.20 - 9.25 "	Concentration E	10.55 - 11.. " — Village Lane
		9.35 - 9.45 "		11.10 - 11.20 "
		9.50 - 10.. "		11.30 - 11.45 "
			O.C. Company visited both batteries. Rainage and the 1st Bn	
			with Regt. in connection with the coming raid. It has been returned from Weather fine.	

Army Form C. 2118.

WAR DIARY
or
INTELLIGENCE SUMMARY.
(Erase heading not required.)

Page V

Instructions regarding War Diaries and Intelligence Summaries are contained in F. S. Regs., Part II. and the Staff Manual respectively. Title pages will be prepared in manuscript.

Place	Date	Hour	Summary of Events and Information	Remarks and references to Appendices
BONNELIEU.	Sept 10		The following concentrations were fired last night.	Map 57cSE 1/10000
		8.45 – 9.15 pm	10.5 – 10.15 pm ⎫ Cross Roads	
		9.10 – 9.15 "	10.35 – 10.45 " ⎬ LA VACQUERIE	
		9.20 – 9.30 "	11.10 – 11.15 " ⎪ R.15.D.95.40.	
		9.40 – 9.50 "	11.35 – 11.40 pm ⎭	
			O.C. company visited the line in the morning. Weather fine	
	11th		The following reliefs took place last night.	
			No 1 Section relieves No 4 Section who returned to Company H.Q.	
			No 2 Section changes places with No 3 Section.	
			O.C. company visited the 15th Welsh and made arrangements for the Situation orders, a copy is attached as Appendix III	
			Arrangements re intercommunication were made with the Fire Support Mess	
			Officer. Weather fine	
	12th		The following concentrations were fired last night	
		8.45 – 8.50	9.40 – 10 ⎫ Cross Roads	
		9.- – 9.10	10.10 – 10.15 ⎬ LA VACQUERIE	
		9.15 – 9.25	10.20 – 10.40 ⎪ Rise 95 60.	
		9.30 – 9.40	10.45 – 11 ⎪	
			11.15 – 11.35 ⎭	

Army Form C. 2118.

WAR DIARY
or
INTELLIGENCE SUMMARY.
(Erase heading not required.)

Page VI

Place	Date	Hour	Summary of Events and Information	Remarks and references to Appendices
CONNEUIL	12th		Information was received that the raid arranged for tonight was postponed indefinitely. O.C. Company visited O.C. 14 R.W.F. and made arrangements with him for the raid on BARRIER TRENCH tomorrow night. Orders were issued for this and a copy is attached as Appendix III. Information was received from O.C. 137 Field Ambulance that 10 O.R. of this Company had been evacuated with Spotted Fever. All the necessary arrangements for isolation of the team were made pending further instructions. O.C. Company visited the 14th Welsh in the evening and arranged for 2 guns to be placed at the rear of FUSILIER TRENCH to fire on the Boche front line should they be wanted by the Infantry who were doing a small raid on FARM TRENCH. Weather Fine	ADDO BOUZEAUCOURT

Army Form C. 2118.

WAR DIARY
or
INTELLIGENCE SUMMARY.
(Erase heading not required.)

Page VII

Place	Date	Hour	Summary of Events and Information	Remarks and references to Appendices
GONNELIEU	13th		The following concentrations were fired last night.	Added GOUZEAUCOURT
		8.45 – 9 pm	⎫	
		9.10 – 9.15 "	⎬ Concentration A.	
		9.20 – 9.30 "		
		9.40 – 9.50 "	⎭	
		10.5 – 10.15	⎫ Cross Roads	
		10.35 – 10.45	⎬	
		11.10 – 11.15	⎬ LA VACQUERIE	
		11.35 – 11.40	⎭ R15c.9½.4.0.	
			4 guns under Lt DUNN fired on FARM TRENCH.	
			O.C. Company visited the line in the morning.	
			At 9.30 pm guns were in their positions for the raid and	
			O.C. Company went to Advanced Battalion HQ. The Left party	
			had considerable difficulty in getting their Bangalore into	
		14th	1.35 am	position so that it was not till 1.35 am that the SM	
			Barrage started. All guns fired well. The raid was unfortunately	
			not successful and guns returned to their positions at 2am.	
			Runners fired A1030. Weather rather wet.	

WAR DIARY
or
INTELLIGENCE SUMMARY.
(Erase heading not required.)

Army Form C. 2118.

Page VIII

Place	Date	Hour	Summary of Events and Information	Remarks and references to Appendices
GONNEHEM	15.		The following which took place last night. No.4 Section relieves No.2 Section No.3 " " " interchanged with No.4 Section	BOUZEAUCOURT Floral Sheet.
	16th		Pt Evans reported sick and 2/Lt Dunn went to the Transport as T.O. 2/Lt Linden taking over No.2 Section temporarily. O.C. Company visited the line. Weather fine. The following concentrations were fired last night. 8·40 - 8·50 9·5 - 9·15 9·25 - 9·35 9·40 - 9·45 } concentration A 10· - 10·10 10·20 - 10·40 10·50 - 11·5 11·15 - 11·30 11·35 - 11·45 } Village Rome. O.C. Company visited the line, and attended a conference at Coy H.Q. with reference to a proposed raid which 32 Machine guns would be employed. The company in reserve being	

Army Form C. 2118.

Page IX

WAR DIARY
or
INTELLIGENCE SUMMARY.
(Erase heading not required.)

Instructions regarding War Diaries and Intelligence Summaries are contained in F. S. Regs., Part II. and the Staff Manual respectively. Title pages will be prepared in manuscript.

Place	Date	Hour	Summary of Events and Information	Remarks and references to Appendices
GONNELIEU	16		Prepared for the future.	
	17th		Plans were prepared for the Machine Gun Scheme for the raid. Weather fine.	MR
			The following concentrations were fired last night	
			8.40 – 8.50 9.5 – 9.15 9.20 – 9.25 9.35 – 9.45 } Concentration A	
			10. – 10.15 10.15 – 10.25 10.30 – 10.40 10.55 – 11.5 11.15 – 11.25 11.35 – 11.45 } Trench Tramway & SONNET FARM.	
			O.C. Company visited 120 Coy in connection with the proposed raid at 3pm. Information was received that the raid has been cancelled. Weather fine.	MR
	18th		The following concentrations were fired last night 8.40 – 8.50 9.0 – 9.10 9.15 – 9.30 9.35 – 9.45 } Concentration E 10. – 10.20 10.30 – 10.50 11.5 – 11.25 11.30 – 11.45 } from Trench R.16.c	MR

WAR DIARY
or
INTELLIGENCE SUMMARY.
(Erase heading not required.)

Army Form C. 2118.

Place	Date	Hour	Summary of Events and Information	Remarks and references to Appendices
GOUZEAU COURT	18th		The Company moved into new Buy huts at GOUZEAUCOURT STATION last night. O.C. Coy visited the line and saw Egyptian Wether fine.	
	19th		The following relief took place last night. No 2 Section relieved No 3 Section who returned to H.Q. No 1 Section changed over with No 4 Section. O.C. Company visited the line in the morning and the Transport in the afternoon. Registration was attempted in the morning on the CAMBRAI ROAD but was not successful. A great deal of movement was witnessed but it was all out of range.	
	20		The following concentrations were fired last night 9.30 - 9.40 10 - 10.20 } BONNET FARM & 8.45 - 9 10.25 - 10.40 } TRENCH TRAMWAY. 9.25 - 9.30 } Concentration A 10.50 - 11 11.15 - 11.35	

Army Form C. 2118

Page XI

WAR DIARY
or
INTELLIGENCE SUMMARY
(Erase heading not required.)

Instructions regarding War Diaries and Intelligence Summaries are contained in F.S. Regs., Part II. and the Staff Manual respectively. Title Pages will be prepared in manuscript.

Place	Date	Hour	Summary of Events and Information	Remarks and references to Appendices
GOUZEAUCOURT	9th		Registration was attempted during the day with success on to CORNER REDOUBT. Sentries were fired at and seen to duck. O.C. Company visited the line. Weather fine. The following concentrations were fired last night. 8.30 – 8.35 / 8.45 – 8.50 / 9.– – 9.10 / 9.15 – 9.25 } Concentration C. 9.45 – 10.– / 10.10 – 10.30 / 10.35 – 10.45 / 10.55 – 11.20 } New work at SONNET FARM.	1000 Shrapnel
do	21st		Day firing was carried out on to CORNER REDOUBT and the CAMBRAI ROAD. Arrangements were made and guns got into position for an operation which the 120 Inf Bde were carrying out this evening about 7pm. Fell thro' this was put thro' till tomorrow. O.C. Company visited the line four times. Weather fine. Shells cast night in conjunction with the artillery. Concentrations were fires 10. – 10.5 pm / 11. – 11.5 pm / 2.– am } Divisional concentration B.15.6, 9.5.	
	22nd			

Army Form C. 2118

Page XII

WAR DIARY
or
INTELLIGENCE SUMMARY
(Erase heading not required.)

Place	Date	Hour	Summary of Events and Information	Remarks and references to Appendices
COURCELOURT	Sept. 22		O.C. Company visited the line in the morning. Four guns cooperated in a most successful raid carried out by the 120 Inf Bde on our right. 2 copies of orders for this are attached. 27000 rounds were fired.	20000 37.86 Appendix IV
	23rd		Lt Spurrell rejoined the Company from leave. Weather very fine. The following reliefs took place last night. No 3 Section relieves No 1 Section who returned to Headquarters. No 2 Section interchanges with No 4 Section. The O.C. Coy went round the line with the G.O.C. 11 elect Battery preparing under the new lottery scheme. O.C. Coy arranged details for a coming raid with 121 M.G. Coy. Weather fine.	
	24th		The following concentrated guns were fired last night.	

WAR DIARY or INTELLIGENCE SUMMARY

Army Form C. 2118

Page 8111

Place	Date	Hour	Summary of Events and Information	Remarks and references to Appendices

GOUZEAUCOURT	24th	8:30 – 8:40
		8:45 – 8:50
		8:55 – 9:
		9:10 – 9:15
			Concentration A. 9:20 – 9:25 SONNET FARM.
			                9:35 – 9:45 Trent Tramway.
			                9:55 – 10:20
			                10:40 – 10:55
			                11:5 – 11:15	

			O.C. confirm centre of the line. M.G.R breathe very free. The following concentrations were fires last night	

	25th	9:5 – 8:15
		8:20 – 8:25
		8:35 – 8:40
		8:50 – 9:-
			Concentration E 9:15 – 9:30
			                9:45 – 9:55 Junction of Trenches
			                10:5 – 10:20 R.16.a.
			                10:35 – 10:55 Cross La VACQUERIE.	

			The enemy shells the vicinity of GOUZEAUCOURT STATION this morning and afternoon with 8 in. 5·9 in. and 4·2's. 10 of our guns were in position in 6:30 hrs for the Right Regt rams and fired from 7:33 hrs to 8:40 hrs. 41000 rounds were fired. The raid was successful although the enemy exploded it as he has withdrawn from his front line and put down a heavy	

1875. Wt. W593/826 1,000,000 4/15 J.B.C. & A. A.D.S.S./Forms/C. 2118.

Army Form C. 2118.

WAR DIARY
or
INTELLIGENCE SUMMARY.
(Erase heading not required.)

Page XIV

Place	Date	Hour	Summary of Events and Information	Remarks and references to Appendices
BOUZEAUCOURT	25th		Barrage on our Front Line from 7.26 to 8.15 p.m. The company has 4 casualties - both slightly wounded.	Map Special Pkt Lossers
	26th		Lt Burnett proceeded on leave to the U.K. The night firing was from last night. 5 prisoners and 1 Machine gun were captured in the raid. O.C. company interviewed were the line, in the morning.	M.R. M.R.
	27th		The following reliefs took place last night. No 1 Sec relieves No 4 Section who returns to H.Q. No 2 Co changes round with No 3 Section. Weather fine.	M.C.
	28th		The following concentrations were fired last night Trench Tramway &	

8 - 8.10
8.15 - 8.20   9 - 9.20
9.30 - 9.45   9.25 - 9.40
                   9.45 - 9.50
Concentration A   10 - 10.15
                   10.25 - 10.45

WAR DIARY
or
INTELLIGENCE SUMMARY.

Army Form C. 2118.

Page XV

Place	Date	Hour	Summary of Events and Information	Remarks and references to Appendices
GOUZEAUCOURT	28		O.C. Company visited the line during the morning. Weather fine	Present Place Aero N.E.S.E.
	29		The following concentrations were fired last night:- 8.- 8.10 8.15 - 8.20 } Concentration E. 8.15 - 8.30 8.25 - 8.40 8.50 - 8.55 } Concentration F. 9.- 9.05 9.15 - 9.30 9.40 - 9.55 } BONNET FARM 10.10 - 10.15 10.25 - 10.35 } Junction of 10.40 - 10.45 } tracks O.C. Company visited the Trenchwork in the morning and at the line at night. Weather fine.	MAP MAP
	30		The following concentrations were fired last night:- 4.- 9.01 8.- 8.10 8.15 - 8.25 } Concentration B. Sunken Lane Concentration 8.30 - 8.35 8.50 - 8.55 9.15 - 9.20 9.30 - 9.50 } Copp Coy 10.- 10.25 } LA BACQUERIE 10.30 - 10.40 } VILLAGE LANE Tracks of Tramway R.15 & R.16a. O.C. Company went to the line in the morning. At DESSART & O.R. returned from CAMIERS	MAP

WAR DIARY
or
INTELLIGENCE SUMMARY.

(Erase heading not required.)

Army Form C. 2118.

Ambulance

Strength of Company Sept 1.   10 Off 181 O.R.
"   "   "   Sept 30   9 " 182 "

Strength Increase During Month
    R.S.M. Stallion from Hospital

Strength Decrease "   "   1 O.R.
    Lt Evans (Lt.) & 1 O.R.

Casualties.   3 O.R Wounded.

Evac's.   Lt P. Dexter & 1 O.R to Camiers.
          Lt Harkness   & 1 O.R to Amiens Camouflage School.

No of Wounds filed during month.   196,000 rounds.

SECRET

Appendix II   War Diary

OPERATION ORDERS No 5

BY CAPT. D. T. AMERY-PARKES
COMMANDING 119th M.G.Coy

11-9-17

Reference map 1/20000 GOUZEAUCOURT Special Sheet.

1. On the night 12/13 the 18th Bn. Welsh Reg are raiding the enemy trenches from R15c 5264 to R15c 9764
2. The 119th M.G. Coy will cooperate with 12 guns
3. Dispositions

    2 guns of No 2 Section under Lt ANDERTON will fire from about R14d 62.68 on to the objective from R15c 4466 to R15d 0566 Time zero to zero+1. From zero+1 to zero+15 they will switch to R15c 3088 to R15d 0005.

    No 1 Section will take up position about R21c 3520 and fire a barrage on R15d 32.92 to R15d 4462 to R15d 3840. Time zero to zero+25.

    No 4 Section will take up position in the I.F. positions and fire from R15d 3944 to R21b 98.90 Time zero to zero+28

    No 3 Section will carry out the ordinary night firing (2 guns) on to targets ① Cross Roads R15d.9862
    ② " " R16c 0205

    Time 8.30 till raid is finished.

4. Guns are to be in position as soon after dusk as possible.
5. Position of Coy H.Q. will be notified later. SEC HQ FARM RAVINE
6. Zero time will be notified later.
7. The following codes will be used

A.A.A.	= Cease fire
B.B.B	= Raid washed out return to Battle positions
C.C.C.	= Commence firing
P.P.P. ( )	= Postpone Zero. (No of minutes after)
D.D.D. ( )	= Continue firing (No of minutes after)

Appendix II

Times will be notified in the following code.

   P = 10 PM
   Q = 11 PM   A = 15 minutes
   R = 12 PM   B = 30 minutes
   S = 1 AM   C = 45 minutes
   T = 2 AM
   U = 3 AM

So that if the barrage is to start at 11.15 pm the following will be sent through the phone

   Q.Q.Q, Q.C.

and if the barrage is to continue for 40 minutes it will be followed by 0.0.0.40

8. Guns will be in position as soon after dusk as possible
9. Flashes must be screened.
10. Night firing boxes and clinometers to be used.
11. Acknowledge.

                                    DH Amery Parkes.
                                          Capt
2.30 pm   O.C. 119 M.G. Coy.

Appendix III War Diary

SECRET

OPERATION ORDER.   No 6
BY CAPT. D.T. AMERY-PARKES.
CMD; 119TH MG COY

12-9-17

Map GOUZEAUCOURT Special Sheet 1/20,000

1. On the night 13th/14th SEP; the 19th Bn R.W.F. are raiding the BARRIER TRENCH 250x each side of the CAMBRAI ROAD.

2. The 119th MG COY. will cooperate with 12 guns.

3. Dispositions

   No 2 section and 2 guns. of No 4 section under LT. HARKNESS will fire from approx; R14d 5565 and will barrage from R22a 3070 to R22d 1070

   Two guns No 3 section (R1 & R2) and 2 guns of No 1 section (MG3 & MG4) under LT ANDERTON from the I.F. position will barrage from R21b 5532 to R22a 3070

   2 guns of No 3 section (R3 & R4) will carry out the ordinary night firing on (1) Cross Roads R16a 0540
   (2) Tramway R15d 8073
   from 8.30 PM till raid is finished.

4. O.C. Coy will be at Right Coy HQ (FOSTERS AVENUE R20d 8015).

5. There will be no specified Zero hour and all orders re firing will come through on the phone or by message.

6. Communication will be established as follows.

   No 2 Section from R14d 5565 will be connected to Infty Coy HQ. in FARM RAVINE and from there to FOSTERS AVENUE

   The I.F. positions will be connected to FOSTERS AVENUE direct

   LT. HARKNESS and LT ANDERTON will send 2 runners each from their gun positions to report to O.C. Coy at FOSTERS AVENUE at 9-30 PM.

7. The following code will be used over the telephone
   A.A.A   - Cease fire
   B.B.B   - Raid washed out return
   C.C.C   - Commence fire
   D.D.D   - Continue firing (no of minutes after)

Appendix III

8. Telephone communication will be arranged where possible.

9. Each section will supply 2 runners for O.C. Coy. Further arrangements to this later.

10. Flashs must be screened.

11. Clinometers and a night firing boxes to be used.

12. Acknowledge.

JHClements? Capt
O.C. 119 M. G. Coy

3 pm

SECRET   **Appendix IV**   Copy No 8.

40TH. DIVISIONAL MACHINE GUN COMPANY.
OPERATION ORDER No 21.
By Captain M.C. Cooper
O.C. 40th. Divisional M.G. Coy.

---

1. The 14th. Battn. Highland Light Infantry will raid the enemy's front line trench from R.8.d.6.7 to R.8.d.15.95 and the road from R.8.d.6.7 to R.8.b.75.08.
If the wind is favourable for smoke barrage, the raid will take place before dark.

2. The 40th. Divisional Machine Gun Company in cooperation with the 119th. and 120th. Machine Gun Companies divided into 6 groups will bring barrage fire to bear as per attached map. The groups are as under:—

Group No	No of Guns	Company	Approximate Gun Position.	Target.
No 1	4	120th	Q.12.c.9.8	From R.8.a.66.48 To R.8.b.0.5.
No 2	4	120th	Q.12.d.3.4	From R.8.b.3.5. To R.8.b.90.55.
No 3	2	40th.Div.	R.14.a.4.0.	X Roads in R.C.3.
No 4	2	40th.Div.	R.13.c.8.5.	Goodman's Farm.
No 5	2	119th.		R.9.c.80.15
No 6	2	119th.		From R.9.c.0.6 To R.9.a.17.18.

TIME OF FIRING: ZERO TO ZERO + 50 MINUTES.
RATE OF FIRING: 150 ROUNDS PER MINUTE.

3. Officers commanding groups will select gun positions in area allotted and have lines laid out and night firing boxes in position on the night previous to the raid.

4. All guns to be laid by clinometer and frequently checked during firing. Report when guns are in position to 40th. Div. M.G Company H.Q. on Beaucamp-Villers Road by code word "RYTO."

all guns to be in position and ready by 6 P.M. on the day fixed.

6. All reports and messages to 40TH. DIV. M.G. COMPANY H.Q.
One orderly to be with each group and one orderly from each group to be at 40TH DIV. M.G. COMPANY H.Q.
In the case of groups being isolated and orderlies not possible a wire will be laid to nearest Infantry Company H.Q.

7. Watches to be synchronized at BATTALION H.Q. (L.G.) R.13.a.8.4. on the day fixed at 4 P.M.

8. Date and hour to be notified later.

9. Arrangements will be made by Officers commanding groups for filling belts.

10. The following Code will be used in connection with the operation:-

    Code word for enterprise   GAY CRUSADER
    Conditions unfavourable   KINGSTON BLACK
    Enterprise will take place   BAYARDO
    Enterprise postponed until
    tomorrow   GAY LAURA

11. Acknowledge.

                                      [signature]

                                     Capt.
                       O.C. 40TH. DIVISIONAL M.G. COMPANY

Copy No. 1 to 120TH. INF. BDE.
Copy No. 2, 3, 4 & 5 to BATTALIONS.
   " No. 6 to D.M.G.O.
   " No. 7 " OFFICE.
   " No. 8 " O.C. 119 M.G. COY.
   " No. 9 " O.C. 120 M.G. COY.
   " No. 10, 11, 12, 13, 14 and 15 to GROUP COMMANDERS.
   " No. 16 to O.C. 120TH. T.M.B.
   " No. 17, 18 and 19 — WAR DIARY.

SECRET.

40TH. DIVISIONAL MACHINE GUN COMPANY.

ADDITIONS AND AMENDMENTS TO 40TH. DIVISIONAL M.G. COY. OPERATION ORDERS №21, DATED 19-9-1917.

---

2 Guns are added to Group 4.

For time of firing for Groups Nº 4, 5 and 6, read:–
 ZERO – 2' to ZERO + 50'.

Guns at R.3, D1, D2, and D3 will fire as follows:–

	TARGET	TIME OF FIRING.
R.3.	R.1.C. 80.65.	ZERO – 4'
D.1. }	M.G's AT R.1.d.	TO
D.2. }	CENTRAL, AND	ZERO + 10'
D.3. }	R.1.d. 43.09.	

Maurice Cooper
Capt.
O.C. 40TH. DIVISIONAL M.G. COY.

19/9/17

COPIES TO ALL RECIPIENTS OF 40TH. DIV. M.G. COY. OPERATION ORDERS Nº 21.

Appendix IV.

Army Form C. 2118.

WAR DIARY
or
INTELLIGENCE SUMMARY.
(Erase heading not required.)

WAR DIARY
119. MACHINE GUN COMPANY.
OCTOBER 1917.

Copy No. 1

WAR DIARY or **INTELLIGENCE SUMMARY**

Army Form C. 2118.

Place	Date	Hour	Summary of Events and Information	Remarks and references to Appendices
GOUZEAUCOURT	Oct 1.		The following reliefs took place last night. No 4 relieved No 2 Sec. who returned to HQ. No 3 Sec. interchanged with No 1 Sec. A raid was expected last night on the enemy lines out the wire on the Blue Front in several places and had some heavy enemy battery work against our 2 batteries. The night was however quiet. O.C. Company visited the line. Weather fine.	Welsh Regt. BOUZEAUCOURT Patrol sheet [signature]
	Oct 2		The following firing was done last night: 8 - 8.10 / 8.15 - 8.20 / 8.25 - 8.35 / 8.40 - 8.50 } Examination (A) 9 - 9.20 / 9.30 - 9.40 / 9.50 - 10.10 / 10.15 - 10.30 } Trench Tramways. Orders were received that the proposed raid of the 15th Welsh Regt. would take place on the night 5/6th October. O.C. Company visited the line at 121 m. C. Eng in connection with the raid. Weather fine.	[signature]

WAR DIARY
or
INTELLIGENCE SUMMARY.

Army Form C. 2118.

Sheet 2

Place	Date	Hour	Summary of Events and Information	Remarks and references to Appendices
GOUZEAUCOURT	Oct 3		Night firing was carried out on gaps cut by the artillery for the raid with the object of keeping them open for the operation. Orders for the raid on the 5th were issued & copy in attached as appendix	See Appendices II
			O.C. Companies visited the line & both battalions	ALOS
	Oct 4		enemy out. Guns were kept firing on the gaps in the wire all night. Weather dull.	
			O.C. Company visited the line and Brigade.	
	Oct 5		Guns were firing all night to keep the gaps for the raid open. O.C. Companies visited the line.	ALOS
			Guns were winded up for the raid at 6.23. 101 to Coy at up posts who were the CAMBRAI ROAD. and continued fire at 6.40 and	
	9.20,		when the raid opened fire at our lines. Our raiding party had entered the german lines, but owing there were killed and all	
			the [Germans] were taken to duman became. Identification was secured. No has 5 casualties	ALOS

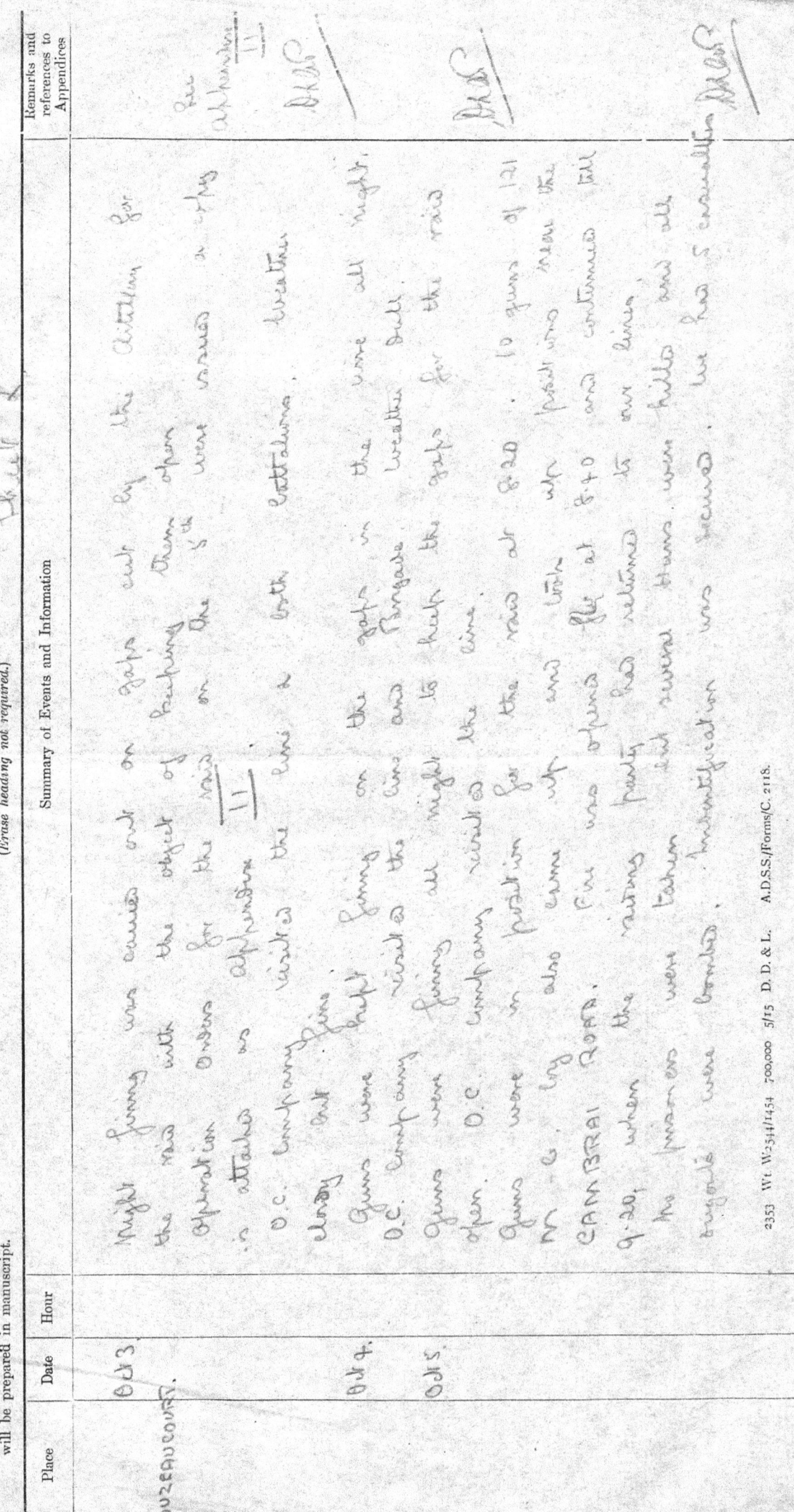

Army Form C. 2118.

WAR DIARY
or
INTELLIGENCE SUMMARY.
(Erase heading not required.)

Page III

Instructions regarding War Diaries and Intelligence Summaries are contained in F. S. Regs., Part II. and the Staff Manual respectively. Title pages will be prepared in manuscript.

Place	Date	Hour	Summary of Events and Information	Remarks and references to Appendices
GOUZEAUCOURT	6/16		Altogether Sgt McCarthy of "A" Coy was hit in the jaw by a MG. Rounds fired 81,500. Orders were received that the Brigade was to be relieved by the Sq Pate 20th Division on the night of the 7/8th and that the Division was going out to rest behind ARRAS. Relief orders and orders for the move & were issued, before an attached an Appendices III and IV . O.C. Sq 2 M-G. Coy came up to arrange relief. Weather wet.	J.R.R.B.
	7/16		Uneventful no A & F wire fires last night. O.C. Company visited all gun positions with O.C. Sq Coy. The Relief commenced at 6.30 pm and was complete by 9 pm which was a very creditable performance considering the weather and state of the ground. After relief the Company proceeded to Huts at HEUDICOURT. Weather very wet and cold.	J.R.R.B.

Army Form C. 2118.

WAR DIARY
or
INTELLIGENCE SUMMARY.
(Erase heading not required.)

Instructions regarding War Diaries and Intelligence Summaries are contained in F. S. Regs., Part II. and the Staff Manual respectively. Title pages will be prepared in manuscript.

Sheet 7.

Place	Date	Hour	Summary of Events and Information	Remarks and references to Appendices
HEUDICOURT	Oct 8th		The company paraded at 1.45 p.m. to march to the Divisional Railhead at RAISON in exchange for Russian PERONNE at 515 p.m. and detrained at S? DENIS at 5 p.m. and marched to huts in the southern portion of PERONNE. The huts were very comfortable and rather scattered.	Ref Map GOZEAUCOURT Sheet 57A MH50
PERONNE	Oct 9th		Inspection very wet all the afternoon. Orders were received that the Brigade would be inspected by General PUTTENEY commanding the III Corps at 3 p.m. The company paraded at 1.45 p.m. and marched down to Victor Square. The General Brigade were drawn up in a hollow square when the General inspected with and gave a short speech after which the Brigade marched past and returned to billets. Weather fine.	MH50
	Oct 10th		The party for the 1st Ammunition Train paraded at 7.30 a.m. and marched down to the station. The Company paraded a training party of 80 men. The train was ¾ of an hour late in getting off	MH50

2353 Wt. W2544/1434 700,000 5/15 D. D. & L. A.D.S.S./Forms/C. 2118.

Army Form C. 2118.

WAR DIARY
or
INTELLIGENCE SUMMARY.
(Erase heading not required.)

Elliot C.

Instructions regarding War Diaries and Intelligence Summaries are contained in F. S. Regs., Part II. and the Staff Manual respectively. Title pages will be prepared in manuscript.

Place	Date	Hour	Summary of Events and Information	Remarks and references to Appendices
PERONNE.	Oct 10th		The entraining was completed at 10 am and the train started at 10.30 am, arriving at BEAUMETZ les RIVIERE'S 4.15 pm. detraining was complete by 6pm. The company marched to billets at MONCHIET, a distance of about 4 miles. The second party arrived at 11.30 pm and was entrained by	A.L.B.
MONCHIET	11th		1.45 am and arrived at BEAUMETZ at 8am getting into billets about 10am.	A.L.B.
			The rest of the men under 2/Lt LORDEN arrived at 2.15 pm. The day was spent in cleaning up and improving billets. Weather fine.	
	Oct 12		The following parades were on to-day. Cleaning guns, kit inspection and improving billets. Recreational Training in the afternoon. Church Parade at SIMENCOURT. Weather fine.	A.L.B.
	13th		Training Programme was commenced a copy is attached as Appendix IV. Weather fine.	
	14th		Training continued	
Oct 15 to 22				A.L.B.

2353 Wt W2544/1434 700,000 5/15 D. D. & L. A.D.S.S./Forms/C. 2118.

Army Form C. 2118.

WAR DIARY
or
INTELLIGENCE SUMMARY.
(Erase heading not required.)

Page 6

Place	Date	Hour	Summary of Events and Information	Remarks and references to Appendices
MONCHIET	Oct 23		Bde. Brigade Scheme for an attack upon a system of Trenches was carried out at SIMENCOURT. Operation Order for the scheme are not attached as appendix V. Weather was very wet.	AAA3
	Oct 24		The Brigade was inspected today on the parade ground by the Brigade Commander who spoke to 19th R.W.F. at SIMENCOURT. Several complimentary remarks upon the turn-out and steadiness of the Company and also of the whole Brigade. O.C. Company left for a Machine Gun Ammunition at CAMIERS. Training continued. Weather locally wet.	AAP
	Oct 25 Oct 26 Oct 27		O.C. Company returned from CAMIERS, locally wet. Both Competitions and Training Ranges were held both were very successful. The syndicate time for the action completion was 25 seconds with 17 hits out of 20 fired on the target. Weather fine.	AAC
	Oct 28		Divine Services were held on the parade ground.	AAC

Army Form C. 2118.

WAR DIARY
or
INTELLIGENCE SUMMARY.
(Erase heading not required.)

Pl. y 7

Instructions regarding War Diaries and Intelligence Summaries are contained in F. S. Regs., Part II. and the Staff Manual respectively. Title pages will be prepared in manuscript.

Place	Date	Hour	Summary of Events and Information	Remarks and references to Appendices
MONCHIET.	29th		Cleaned and greased Company Parade at 7.55 am and marched to HUMBERCOURT a distance of 12 miles. Advance via KARBRET, COUTERELLE & COULLEMONT. The company arrived in billets at 12.30 p.m. O.C. company received a complimentary letter from the General with out of the company.	June 11.
HUMBERCOURT	30th		Training was carried out in the morning. P.T. Arms Drill, Gun Drill and Company drill. In the afternoon the Company went for a run of about 3 miles. Weather fine.	
	31st		O.C. Company attended a conference at Bde. HQ at 9.30 am. The following training was carried out: Gun Drill, Stoppages, Arms Drill, Aiming gun Drill & judging distances Drill. Weather fine.	

2353 Wt. W3544/1454 700,000 5/15 D. D. & L. A.D.S.S./Forms/C. 2118.

Army Form C. 2118.

WAR DIARY
or
INTELLIGENCE SUMMARY.
(Erase heading not required.)

Copy 1

Instructions regarding War Diaries and Intelligence Summaries are contained in F. S. Regs., Part II. and the Staff Manual respectively. Title pages will be prepared in manuscript.

Place	Date	Hour	Summary of Events and Information	Remarks and references to Appendices

	1st to 31st October		October.
			
			APPENDIX 1
			
			Strength of Company Oct 1 10 Off. 162 O.R.
			" " Oct 31st 11 Off. 163 O.R.
			
			CASUALTIES NIL.
			
			COURSES. Sgt PARKER Lo M.G. School SANNERS
			                    2/Lt A. ELLIOT. 1.O.R.
			
			STRENGTH INCREASE Nil.
			           DECREASE
			
			Ammunition Expended - 106000 rounds.	

2353 Wt. W2344/1454 700,000 5/15 D. D. & L. A.D.S.S./Forms/C. 2118.

Appendix II   War Diary

SECRET

OPERATION ORDERS No 7

BY CAPT. D.T. AMERY-PARKER
CMG. 119th M.G.COY

3-10-17

MAP. REF. GOUZEAUCOURT 10,000 Special Sheet.

1. On night 5/6th October the 18th Batt; Welsh Reg are raiding CORNER REDOUBT.

2. The 119th M.G. Coy and 121st M.G. Coy are placing a barrage round the objective

3. Zero hour will be notified later

4. Dispositions of guns.

No of Group	No of Guns	Approx; Position	Targets
1	4	R26 b 4622	BARRACK TRENCH CAMBRAI ROAD to R22 b 30,30
2	6	R26 b 4050	R22 a 0048 to R22 b 6025
3	4	R26 b 2050	Front line from R21 b 5295 to R15 d 3648.
4	4	R21 c 50,00	Trench from R15 a 3648 to R15 a 4476 to R15 a 2898
5	4	R19 d 7050	Front line R22 a 0048 to R21 b 5293
6	2	R14 b 6800	Trenches R15 a 6050 R15 a 9232. R15 a 2898.

5. Rate of fire 150 rounds. per min per gun
6. Time of firing
   Zero to Zero + 40
7. Coy H.Q. for the operation will be at 15 RAVINE
8. Communication
   Each group will send 1 orderly to Coy H.Q. There will be a telephone from 15 RAVINE to RT. SEC;
9. Guns to be in position by 8-30 P.M. and the fact reported to H.Q. by the above orderly.
10. At Zero + 40 guns will stand by till Zero + 60 when they will return to battle positions or billets independently unless orders to the contrary are received
11. Reports on operations to be sent to O.C. Coy the next morning
12. Clinometers to be used and guns frequently checked.
13. All precautions to be taken against gas
14. Acknowledge.

D.H. Amery Parkes
Capt.
O.C. 119 M.G. Coy

Appendix III   War Diary

ORDERS FOR MOVE
119th M.G. COY
Oct 8th 1917

Map Ref

1. LT VANDYKE and CPL READ will report to Town Major PERONNE at 9am for billeting
2. LT HARKNESS and SGT PEARMAN will report to the Staff Captain at PERONNE taking with them rations up to and including the 10th Oct 1917
3. The Transport and Signallers will move at a time to be notified later under the orders of the B.T.O. Transport lines at PERONNE are at I.21.d.15.
4. Personnel will move by bus from HEUDICOURT. time will be notified later
5. Every man will carry a rolled blanket when proceeding to PERONNE

Oct 10th 1917

1. On the 9th Oct a Baggage dump will be established at the entraining station. This will contain blankets rolled in bundles of ten, also surplus or spare kit
2. Time and place of entrainment will be notified later
3. Detraining railhead BEAUMETZ.
4. Billets are at GOUY-EN-ARTOIS.
5. The Company will proceed by 2 trains. Correct dispositions attached
6. Sufficient cord will be provided to secure bicycles to wagons after wagons have been put on flats.
7. Lorries will meet trains on arrival at BEAUMETZ for the conveyance of blankets rolled in bundles of ten.
8. Sections will march from BEAUMETZ to GOUY-EN-ARTOIS distance about 3½ miles

                                    Capt
                              Comd 119th M.G. Coy.

8-10-17

Appendix IV   War Diary

RELIEF ORDERS

SECRET.

By Capt D.J. Amery-Parkes
CMD 119th MG Coy.

Map Ref. GOUZEAUCOURT 1/20,000 Special Sheet.

1. On night 7th/8th Oct the 119th M.G. Coy will be relieved by the 59th M.G. Coy.
2. After relief sections will proceed via CAMBRAI RD to HEUDICOURT. Guides will meet them in the square.
3. Officers of relieving sections will visit section officers on the morning of the 7th inst at about 11am.
4. Relieving sections will be guided up to Sec. H.Q. by guides from Coy H.Q. Rt section will go to CEMETRY DUMP.
5. Guides from gun teams to be at CEMETRY DUMP, 15 RAVINE, and AEROPLANE ALLEY at 8pm.
6. Belt boxes etc will <u>not</u> be handed over.
7. Maps and Trench Stores will be handed over in the usual way receipts being obtained. <u>New</u> water tins to be handed over.
8. Aeroplane sights will not be handed over.
9. Code word for the relief will be FINI which will be wired to H.Q. directly relief is complete.
10. Telephones will be brought out.
11. 2 gun limbers per section will be at ① CEMETRY DUMP No 2 Sec
                                    ② 15 RAVINE   " 4 "
                                    ③ AEROPLANE ALLEY " 1 "

    No 3 Section and H.Q limbers will be at H.Q. at 7pm.
12. Chargers with limbers except C.O's + 2nd in C. at 10pm. 1 horse for Lt VANDYKE at H.Q. at 9AM.
13. Extreme caution must be exercised over the telephone if it is used in connection with the relief.
14. All trenches and emplacements must be clean and free of empties etc which can be sent down tonight.
15. Acknowledge.

                                                                        D.J. Amery-Parkes Capt.
                                                                       O.C. 119 M-G Coy

Appendix VI. War Diary.

ORDERS FOR BRIGADE SCHEME

1. On the 23rd Oct/17 the 119th Infty Bde will carry out a practice attack at K 34. 35 Q 45.

2. The enemy's lines will be attacked on a front of 400ˣ to a depth of 1200ˣ.

3. To achieve this 2 Battalions will take the 1st objective and the 2 other Battalions will pass through them to take the final objective.

4. 119th M.G. Company will co-operate. 1 Section to hold our original F.L. & 3 Sections for barrage work.

5. No 3 Section will hold the original F.L. and will arrange to belt it so as to be able to defend it in case of a failure. This section will be ready to move at a minute's notice and will constitute the Brigade Reserve.

6. Nos 1, 2 & 4 Sections will place a barrage about 450ˣ in front of each objective. They will be divided into 2 groups. No 1 Group consisting of Nos 1 & 2 Sects
   No 2 "   "   " No 4 Sect.
   Group positions are approximately.

6b Barrage guns will open fire on the 1st objective i.e. line C.C. and creep forward to 400ˣ in front of final objective D.D. Where the barrage will become stationery

7. These sections will be ready to move up to the captured position after the objectives have been taken. A carrying party from the infantry will be detailed to assist them in moving.

8. Times of firing.
   ZERO to + 20 Creep from C.C. to 400ˣ beyond.
   FROM Zero + 20 to + 30 remain 400ˣ beyond
   "   "   + 30 to + 40 Creep to final objective D.D.
   "   "   + 40 to + 43 remain on final objective.
   "   "   + 43 to + 46 creep to 400ˣ beyond D.D.
   "   "   + 46 to + 65 remain.

9. Rate of fire 100 rounds per minute per gun.
10. Dumps will be formed at each barrage position and in the FRONT LINE. They will consist of:-
  5 boxes of S.A.A. per gun (imag).
  10 belt boxes
  2 tins of water per gun
  1 tin of oil " "
  1 box of bombs " " (imag)
  2 picks & 2 shovels per gun (")
  Battalion & Bde Dumps will be formed and used in emergency.
11. Should guns move they will take as much of the dump as is practicable with them.
12. Communication
  Each section will detail 2 runners for communication.
13. Messages.
  Dummy are to be sent. These must be correctly made out and sent in an envelope.
14. A German counter-attack will be assimilated by 3 VERY LIGHTS.
15. Officers will use their initiative should the attack be held up, either on the Bde front or its flanks.
16. If gun positions are concealed from the enemy, officers must arrange to place observers out where the progress of the attack can be watched.
17. Dress
  Fighting order. Steel Helmets. S.B.R's & P.H. HELMET
  No 3 of each gun will carry 1 pick
  " 4 "   "   "   "   " 1 shovel.
All other ranks will carry three Sandbags folded up on the back under the equipment.
All other ranks will carry 2 bombs (imag) water bottles filled, Iron Rations.

18. Casualties, will be made by section Officers & men will be given labels to denote their injuries.
19. Synchronisation

20. Pack animals will be used if possible. These will be leads of gun limbers and will be kept ready at the limber park.
21. Parade 8.30 a.m.
22. Clinometers, aiming sticks, and condensers will be used
23. Section Officers will arrange to define the danger area in front of their guns.
24. When guns move forward they will invariably be carried in the trench cases.
25. When Barrage guns have finished their duty they will automatically come up to C.H.Q
26. C.H.Q is at Q.4.a.4.1.
27. When Barrage Guns move forward from C.H.Q, they will only take 50% of Machine Gunners with them, and will use the "carrying party" to make up their numbers. Remaining Mach, Gunners will remain at C.H.Q, whence they will be sent for in the event of casualties.
28. Runners may be taken from the "Carrying Party."

O.C. 119 M.G. Coy

Oct 22

I

War Diary

119 M. G. Coy.

No 1

PERSONNEL FOR TRAINS E.T.C.

BY ROAD.   Nos 3, 6 & 9 LIMBERS.
  7 MULES.
  1 RIDER.
  Sergt. GREY.
  Pte. FERGUSON. R.
  Pte. STANLEY.
  Pte. SCURR.
  Pte. KENNEDY. N.
  4 drivers.

1ST OMNIBUS TRAIN.
  H.Q. LIMBER & No 12 (SIGNALS APPARATUS)
  4 MULES.
  6 RIDERS.
  2 drivers.
  3 grooms.

PERSONNEL.

O.C. COY.

LT. DEXTER.	2/LT. LORDEN.
2/LT. ELLIOTT.	2/LT. SPORRELL.

H.Q. SEC.

C.S.M. STAPLEFORD.	PTE. McCLURE.
PTE. PLAYER.	PTE. DUGGETT.
PTE. WISE.	

No 1 SEC.

SERGT. ROBERTS.	CORPL. WOOD.	L/C MAIDER.
L/C BETT.	L/C KINGHAM.	L/C FISK.
PTE. ASKWITH.	PTE. BADGER.	PTE. BIRD S.
EVANS T.I.	GALE.	HEALEY.
JENKINS H.	McINNES.	PETERS.
PERRY.	WOODWARP. T.	YOUNG A.

3.   2ND TRAIN (CONT)
H.Q. SEC.   — 11 —

C.Q.M.S. HUTCHINSON	SERGT. CAWTHORNE	CORP. METHERELL
CORP. AUSTEN	L/C TAYLOR	L/C MACDONALD
PTE. HEADEN	PTE. CRAM	PTE. MELLSOP
FOX	BAGGOTT	LANGFORD
WHATELEY	DAVIS J.	CRAWFORD
EVANS R.	MARTIN	PAGE
QUINNELL	WATERSON	HOPE
KENWORTHY	PACKHAM	GILLES
THOMAS D.	PUDDICK	

Nº 4 SEC.

SERGT. MACQUEEN	CORPL. BEAUMONT	L/C HODGES
L/C SPICER	L/C STOCKDEN	L/C DAMS
PTE. BURGIN	PTE. BELL	PTE. BROOKS
CARTER	DAINTY	EDWARDS
GREENWOOD J.T.	HOLBROOK	HOYLE
HIGGINSON	HOPE	JOHNSON R.
JACKSON W.	HUNN	REID A.
THURSFIELD	WILCOX	WILSON
CASSIDY	SHINEMAN	CURWEN
GARNER	TINKLER	BRADLEY

ANY DETAILS

2   1ST TRAIN (CONT)

PTE. ROBINSON.   PTE. BARANDALE.   PTE. BANNARD.
     BARKER.   CLARK R.F.   STENNING.

No 2 SEC.

SERGT. DAVIS.   CORP. BEECH.   L/C BENHAM.
L/C HETHERINGTON.   PTE. BLOXHAM.   PTE. BOTTERILL.
PTE. BURNARD.   ELLIOTT.   GREGORY.
     GOULD.   JOHNSON E.   KEEN.
     SULLIVAN.   VARNUM.   WEST.
     WHEELER.   WAUGH.   WILLISON.
     YOUNG W.B.   KNIGHT.   NEATE.
     PENNELL.   WILLIS.   CROMBIE.
     BETTS H.

No 3 SEC.

SERGT. HUNNABALL.   CORP. O'NEILL.   CORP. READ.
L/C WATSON.   L/C WADDELOW.   L/C RICHARDSON.
PTE. TEW.   PTE. TROTMAN.   PTE. IRONSIDE.
     HOOPER.   CLARK. B.   FERGUSON J.D.
     FORSTER.   FRASER.   GREENBANK.
     GIBBS.   GUNNER.   HUGH.
     HALLETT.   KEEPING.   KENNEDY. J.
     LANSDOWNE.   BLOFIELD.   PARK.
     ROBERTS.   STINTON.   WOOD E.

2ND OMNIBUS TRAIN.

Nos 1,2,4,5,7,8,10,11, limbers.
WATER-CART & COOK'S CART.
REMAINING DRIVERS & GROOMS.
        36 MULES.
            LT. ANDERTON (½)
LT. VANDYKE.   2/LT. DODIN.

Army Form C. 2118.

WAR DIARY
or
INTELLIGENCE SUMMARY.
(Erase heading not required.)

War Diary

119th Machine Gun Company

November 1917

Army Form C. 2118.

WAR DIARY
or
INTELLIGENCE SUMMARY.
(Erase heading not required.)

Page 1

Instructions regarding War Diaries and Intelligence Summaries are contained in F. S. Regs., Part II. and the Staff Manual respectively. Title pages will be prepared in manuscript.

Place	Date	Hour	Summary of Events and Information	Remarks and references to Appendices
HUMBERCOURT	1		Training continued in the morning. Coy usually running in the afternoon.	A.W.P.
	2		Capt D. J. Ammerson proceeds on 14 days leave to U.K. Breakfast. Coy company carried out training in skill at arms.	A.W.P.
	3		Afternoon was of chromatic. Afternoon show arm drill. Gunfire. Range Work. Recreational Training.	A.W.P.
	4		Church Parade 11am.	
	5-8		Training continued. 1/ Lt B.E. Anderson proceeded on leave to the U.K. on the evening of the 8th.	
	9		Box Scheme — Word fighting	
	10		Training continued.	
	11		Church Parade	
	12		Brigade Scheme	
	13		Ordinary Training continued and Range Work.	
	14		Brigade Scheme — open fighting.	
	15			
	16		The Company moved from HUMBERCOURT to MONCHIET — leaving at	A.W.P.

Army Form C. 2118.

WAR DIARY
or
INTELLIGENCE SUMMARY.
(Erase heading not required.)

Page 1.

Place	Date	Hour	Summary of Events and Information	Remarks and references to Appendices
MONCHIET	16	6.30 am	and arriving at MONCHIET 10:30 am. Capt Annan Rankin returning from leave.	MAP
GONNIECOURT	17th		The Company left MONCHIET at 6.30 pm and marched to GONNIECOURT arriving in billets about 11 pm. No men fell out on the march.	MAP
	18th		A conference on the coming operations was held at Bn. HQ at 11 am. The company prepared for open fighting.	
BARASTRE	19th		The Company left GONNIECOURT about 9 pm and marched to BARASTRE a distance of about 14 miles. No man fell out. Billets near the Brigade were unsuited. 1 Phono Notice to venue.	MAP
	20th		The bombardment for the front started at 6.20 am. The Company remained at BARASTRE all day.	

WAR DIARY
or
INTELLIGENCE SUMMARY

(Erase heading not required.)

Army Form C. 2118.

Place	Date	Hour	Summary of Events and Information	Remarks and references to Appendices
DOIGNIES	21st		The Company marched to DOIGNIES arriving about 10.30 am and arrived in Bivouacs about 2 P.M. Weather very wet.	App
	22nd		O.C. Company went up & with the C.D.C to recoinnoitre GRAINCOURT and BOURLON WOOD. The Company marched off at 3.30 pm arriving at GRAINCOURT at 11 pm. Orders for the attack on BOURLON WOOD were issued and guns were in position by 6.30 a.m.	App
	23rd		A narrative of the attack is attached as Appendix II.	Appendix II
	25th		Suffered heavy casualties, 1 killed and Killing 19 wounded. On the night of the 27th the remainder of the Brigade were relieved and marched to dug out in the HINDENBURG SUPPORT line behind HAVRINCOURT. 9 limbers had to be left behind as there were no animals to bring them out.	App

Army Form C. 2118.

WAR DIARY
or
INTELLIGENCE SUMMARY.
(Erase heading not required.)

Page IV

Place	Date	Hour	Summary of Events and Information	Remarks and references to Appendices
LECHELLE	26th		The Company marched from HAVRINCOURT to LECHELLE arriving about 6.15 p.m. The Company stables from the Company lines. Weather fine.	MAP
	27th		The Company left billets at 9 a.m. and marched to YPRES Station where we entrained for BEAUMETZ arriving at 3 p.m. The Company then marched to POMMIER arriving about 5.30 p.m.	MAP
POMMIER	28th		The day was spent in cleaning up and improving billets.	
	29th		O.C. Company attended a conference at Divisional H.Q. at 11 a.m. Company training was commenced. The 9 km bus left billets to report to Company. Weather fine.	MAP
	30th		Company training continued. O.C. Coy attended a conference at Bde H.Q. at 11 a.m.	

Appendix I

Strength of Company Nov 1 — 10 Off. 141 O.R.
" " " Nov 30 — 5 " 36 "
Decrease — 4 Off. 45 O.R.
Reinforcements — 2 Off.

Names.
Reginald McQueen
Pte Penny ... Cookery School 3rd Army

CARRIERS

119th Machine Gun Company

Narrative of operations at BOURLON WOOD
Nov 23rd, 24th and 25th

Dispositions for the Attack.

2 Guns were attached to each of the Front Battalions.

12 Guns were detailed to form a right defensive flank to the Brigade to move forward by bounds in echelon.

Guns were got into position in darkness, the right defensive guns taking up positions about F.19.d.9.7. Zero hour was 10.30 a.m. and the guns started moving forward by bounds.

By 12.30 p.m. they were in position along the right edge of the wood in

F.14.d. & across the CAMBRAI ROAD. When moving forward these guns sustained heavy casualties from enfilade M.G., rifle & shell fire from the direction of FONTAINE. 1 Officer was killed, 1 Officer wounded & 24 O.R's killed & wounded 1 gun being knocked out.

About 3 p.m. O.C. Company went down to the line to reorganise the right defensive flank. Guns were placed along the right edge of the wood from F.14.b.3.6. down to the CAMBRAI ROAD. so as to belt the whole right flank. 8 guns were used for this. 1 Section was sent into reserve at ANNEUX

CHAPELLE.

Meanwhile the guns attached to the Battalions had moved forward, the two left guns moving up to positions about F.18.b.1.5. to defend the left flank. These guns remained in this position the whole time. The two right guns moved up to right Bn. H.Q. where they were kept in reserve until the 23rd when they were moved forward into the line. On the 24th the guns on the right flank obtained many good targets on the enemy concentrating round FONTAINE and caused him considerable casualties.

About 2 p.m. a heavy counter attack forced the right of the Bde back. The Machine Guns remained in position till all the Infantry had got back. One gun was surrounded but kept firing till the last minute causing the enemy numerous casualties.

When the Infantry were all back the Machine Guns were swung back to form a defensive line along the CAMBRAI ROAD At the same time a section of 24th M.G. Coy was ordered to belt the ridge behind the CAMBRAI ROAD i/c the 60 contour line in F.20.1 Section of 2nd M.G. COY. was sent up to reinforce at ANNEUX CHAPELLE.

About 6.30 p.m. the situation was restored and the guns reformed on the right defensive flank. The remainder of the night was quiet. On the 25th about 10 a.m. the enemy delivered heavy counter-attacks against our line in the wood. The reserve section of M.G's was therefore sent up to belt the main Ride running E to W. through the wood. This was successfully done and the guns were relieved in those positions that night.

M Ament Parkes.

Nov 29th
O.C 119th Capt. M.G. Coy.

Army Form C. 2118.

WAR DIARY
or
INTELLIGENCE SUMMARY.
(Erase heading not required.)

Vol 19

War Diary

119th Machine Gun Coy.

Dec 1917

Army Form C. 2118.

WAR DIARY
or
INTELLIGENCE SUMMARY.
(Erase heading not required.)

PAUL

Instructions regarding War Diaries and Intelligence Summaries are contained in F. S. Regs., Part II. and the Staff Manual respectively. Title pages will be prepared in manuscript.

Place	Date	Hour	Summary of Events and Information	Remarks and references to Appendices
POMMIER	1.		The Company received orders to move at 11.30 am. than never subsequently cancelled and notification was received that the Brigade would relieve the 47th Bn. 16 Division in the BULLECOURT SECTOR tomorrow.	PAW
	2.		The Company moved by bus from POMMIER to ERVILLERS, thence into the line to relieve the 47th M.G. Coy. Relief was complete by 11.30 pm. 13 gun positions were taken over and tripods so as to put at a protective barrage in front of the Infantry. Company HQ at ST LEGER Sq. B. 2.4.	PAW
ST LEGER	3		O.C Coy visited all guns & Bn HQ. Enemy very quiet no night firing was carried out by request of O.C. Rt Bn. Weather fine.	PAW
	4		O.C Coy went round the line with the D.M. G.O. and arranged several alterations with regard to the Barrage & Battle lines. Enemy quiet.	PAW

Army Form C. 2118.

WAR DIARY
or
INTELLIGENCE SUMMARY.
(Erase heading not required.)

Sheet 3.

Place	Date	Hour	Summary of Events and Information	Remarks and references to Appendices
Br KEGER.	9.		244 M.C. Coy on the W.R. Sec. O.C. Company went round the line with O.C. 244 M.C. Coy. weather wet	AKeB
	10.		No 1 Section No 2 Section was relieved by 244 M.C. Coy by 7 p.m. After relief the Company returned to camp at ERVILLERS. During the night orders came in that the Company was to stand to at 6.30 am on an attack by the enemy was expected.	AKeB
ERVILLERS.	11		The Company stood to at from 6.30 am to 6.45 am after which it was ready at ½ hrs notice at 5 minutes notice till 8.30 am after which ½ hr notice. As per Brigade Orders. Nothing unusual occurred.	AKeB
	12.		Stand to was at 6.30 as before. At 6.50 the enemy opened a heavy Barrage on the Rase on our right. No orders came through and the situation quietened down about 8.30 am. The Company received orders to move.	AKeB

Walter [signature] Major

Army Form C. 2118.

WAR DIARY
or
INTELLIGENCE SUMMARY.

Sheet 2

(Erase heading not required.)

Instructions regarding War Diaries and Intelligence Summaries are contained in F. S. Regs., Part II and the Staff Manual respectively. Title pages will be prepared in manuscript.

Place	Date	Hour	Summary of Events and Information	Remarks and references to Appendices
ST LEGER	5th		O.C. Company visited the line. Requirements for the Company arrived. 28 N.D. posts and 3 maps. Night firing was carried out on known ten behind the enemy lines.	AAR
	6th		4000 rds being fired. O.C. Company visited the line in the morning and made arrangements to attack 2 guns to O.C. Left Battalion for the defence of the ANVERNE. Emergency positions were chosen for these guns.	AAR
	7th		Night firing was carried out on tracks and roads behind the enemy lines. O.C. by road to the en. at night.	AAR
	8th		O.C. Company visited the Transport lines & Q.M. Stores. Situation quiet, weather wet.	OR
	9th		Orders were received that the Company would be relieved by the	

Army Form C. 2118.

WAR DIARY
or
INTELLIGENCE SUMMARY.
(Erase heading not required.)

Page 4.

Place	Date	Hour	Summary of Events and Information	Remarks and references to Appendices
ERVILLERS.	13.		Stand to was at 6.30 am as the previous day. At 4 pm orders were received that the Company would reinforce the line front immediately. O.C. went ahead to Brigade H.Q. and the following dispositions were decided upon: 2 guns in not at U.20 central. 4 guns in VALLEY TRENCH. 5 " in RAILWAY RESERVE as Brigade Reserve. No 2 Section remained in its position. Company H.Q. with the Subsection in RAILWAY RESERVE.	
RAILWAY. U.25.a.7.4.	14.		O.C. Company visited the guns in the line. Situation quiet.	
	15.		Orders were received that the 19th R.W.F. would carry out a minor operation against NEPTUNE TRENCH U.21.a. with the object of killing the enemy, destroying the dugouts and trench and subsequently to dig a strong post on the viainity of junction NEPTUNE-TRIDENT. The Company	

WAR DIARY or INTELLIGENCE SUMMARY

Army Form C. 2118.

Page 5

Place	Date	Hour	Summary of Events and Information	Remarks and references to Appendices
	15		Put up a barrage with 13 guns; fire on CORPSE TRENCH, TRIDENT ALLEY, BEEF ALLEY and sunken road in VII Sec. The operation was entirely successful, 2 Prisoners being taken and went to enemy failed.	MAP
	16/17		Relieved. Quiet. Weather very wet.	RUP.
	18.		Orders were received that the Company would relieve the 244 M.G. Coy in the normal gun positions tomorrow. Situation quiet.	
	19.		The Company relieved 244 M.G. Coy by 12 midday. All positions were the same as previously held. Situation quiet.	
	20.-24.		Situation quiet. Nothing unusual to report. Night firing was carried out each night on selected targets and on the 23rd a party of the enemy were engaged with direct fire and dispersed.	

Army Form C. 2118.

WAR DIARY
or
INTELLIGENCE SUMMARY.

Page 6.

(Erase heading not required.)

Place	Date	Hour	Summary of Events and Information	Remarks and references to Appendices
ST LEGER.	25.		O.C. Company went to the line.	
	26.		Fine and weather very cold some snow	
	27.		Weather cold	
	28.		O.C. Coy & 2 i/c went and had a look at R.E. dump.	
	29.		Orders were received that we by 11.15 hrs.	
	30.		to report to O.C. 174th M.G. Coy at BIHUCOURT	
	31.			

Army Form C. 2118.

WAR DIARY
or
INTELLIGENCE SUMMARY.
(Erase heading not required.)

Vol 20

War Diary
119th M G Company
January 1918

WAR DIARY
or
INTELLIGENCE SUMMARY.
(Erase heading not required.)

Army Form C. 2118.

Place	Date	Hour	Summary of Events and Information	Remarks and references to Appendices
ERVILLERS	1.		The Company had baths and went to DE LIGER for trench post treatment. Weather very cold.	
	2.		Information was received that the Coys Commanders would inspect the Company and transport. Commenced at 8.45 pm. All tents were filled and overhauled. Weather cold.	NJW
	3.		The Coys Commander inspected the company. The inspection went satisfactorily. Weather still cold. After the inspection went No 3 Section went into the line to relieve No 4 Section who returned to billets about 7.30 pm.	NJW
	4.		Training was carried out. Subjects - Bayonet - Gun Drill - Bore Ripkord Drill. Weather cold.	NJW
	5.		Training continued. Subjects - Stoppages - mechanism - lecture indirect fire. Sentence of 21 days FP No1 on Pte Nunn promulgated on parade. O.C. Company went that afternoon line of the division with the Cmdt N.C.O	NJW

WAR DIARY or INTELLIGENCE SUMMARY

Army Form C. 2118.

Hal 3

Place	Date	Hour	Summary of Events and Information	Remarks and references to Appendices
St Leger	8		Machine Gunnery. Weather cold. At about 6.30 am the S.O.S. was sent up from the entire Brigade front. The enemy attacked with flammenwerfer and succeeded in entering our front trench. He was dressed up to appear as a counter attack during which he left 18 prisoners in our hands. The rest of the day and night were quiet. Weather cold.	SAP
	9		Relieved. Quiet, weather cold	SAP
	10		O.C. Company returned from the Flying Corps. Relieved on quiet. Weather. Thaw began today and now west.	SAP
	11		O.C. Company visited the line and the situation. Men fine was carried out on trains and motor lorries up to enemy front line. Information having been received that the enemy was	SAP

Army Form C. 2118.

WAR DIARY
or
INTELLIGENCE SUMMARY.
(Erase heading not required.)

Instructions regarding War Diaries and Intelligence Summaries are contained in F. S. Regs., Part II. and the Staff Manual respectively. Title pages will be prepared in manuscript.

Place	Date	Hour	Summary of Events and Information	Remarks and references to Appendices
CRUVILLERS	11.		Re Carrying out a relief of 9 p.m.	Ply +
	12.		O.C. Company visited the line. Stand to at 3 a.m. Sent Lt Curr Shilling	
			and Queens Lane and KNUCKLE AVENUE. Weather warm.	
	13.		Lt CHRISTIE + 4 O.R.'s to take over the duties of Tunnelling	
			Officer was was taken on the strength by the Company as	
			attached. 4 O.R. from the Company were transferred to 181	
			Machine Gun Company + 2 O.R. to 3RD Machine Gun Company	
			to replace the strength of Companies in the Division.	
			Night fairly warm carried out on tasks and trades between	
			the forming up and R/r action. Quiet + weather colder.	
	14.		O.C. Company visited the line. Bomb. / work. was commenced	N.P.
			on C. Battn. front at OT. 24. D. 75. 90. 4 Employees ents	

Army Form C. 2118.

WAR DIARY
or
INTELLIGENCE SUMMARY.

(Erase heading not required.)

Blur S.

Place	Date	Hour	Summary of Events and Information	Remarks and references to Appendices
RUGEE	14.		4 shelters are being built here & men on two shifts daily are sorting the work over.	PUC
	15.		Night firing was as usual. Better protection was continued. Night firing was carried out on wider scale and wider. Weather not satisfactory. Quiet.	PUC
	16.		After the recent heavy rain of the trenches have commenced to fall in all available men were put on building them. O.C. company never gave employment and orders were given until to the dug outs already stated. No night work was actually difficult to get formed up, all movement was carried out at night. It was thought to later Hame. NCR the	PUC

A 7092]. Wt. w1289/M129r. 750,000. 1/17. D, D & L., Ltd. Forms/C2118/14.

Army Form C. 2118.

WAR DIARY
or
INTELLIGENCE SUMMARY.
(Erase heading not required.)

Page 6

Place	Date	Hour	Summary of Events and Information	Remarks and references to Appendices
ST LEGER	16		Unable to see any firing. Weather mild. The enemy shelled any movement by day.	
	17.		Owing to the state of the ground and trenches near the new British Patrols it was decided to stop work on it and to start on the other side of the Quéant road, which is lighter, much nearer and free Shelling of RAILWAY RESERVE & QUEENT LANE.	
	18		O.C. Company visited the right Lines and fired the Lewis Gun from Sgt. E. Batting's position. Fairly quiet with the Gun.	
	19		O.C. Company visited the trenches in the morning and the line at night. Some shelling of RAILWAY RESERVE and CRUX ROAD	

WAR DIARY or INTELLIGENCE SUMMARY

Army Form C. 2118.

Page 7

Place	Date	Hour	Summary of Events and Information	Remarks and references to Appendices
St KEGER	19		During the evening our guns were active at 6 a.m. sweeping enemy roads and tracks. Weather fair.	RMP
	20		Situation Quiet. Lt J.E. EDWARDES proceeded on leave to the U.K. Weather fair. At 10 a.m. the right gun in Valley Tr saw 3 enemy & opened fire. 1 hit was observed, the others & stretchers O.C. Company visits the line. The mean wenders have been	RMP
	21		given charge of mud and are favorable. A conference of Machine Gun Company Commanders was held at Company Hd at 7 p.m. Situation quiet. Weather rather wet.	RMP
	22		Work was commenced on the permanent Battery position at T.24.b.60.80. A working party of 5 men is being provided	RMP

Army Form C. 2118.

WAR DIARY
or
INTELLIGENCE SUMMARY.

Page 8.

(Erase heading not required.)

Place	Date	Hour	Summary of Events and Information	Remarks and references to Appendices
ST LEGER	22		Day was for the first few days. O.C. Company visited the line. Weather fair.	Map
	23		2/Lt SPURRELL rejoined from leave. O.E, Cay visited O.C. 121 m.g. Company. The usual night firing was carried out last night. Weather fair. Situation Quiet.	Map
	24		O.C. Company went to the line. Night firing was carried out last night as usual. Weather fine. Situation Quiet.	Map
	25		Capt GOTON proceeded on leave to the U.K. O.C. Company went to the line. Night firing was carried out as usual. Last night 2/Lt DEXTER was admitted to Hospital sick. Situation fairly active. Considerable shelling.	Map

Army Form C. 2118.

WAR DIARY
or
INTELLIGENCE SUMMARY.
(Erase heading not required.)

Page 9

Place	Date	Hour	Summary of Events and Information	Remarks and references to Appendices
KEGER	25		of front and back areas	
	26.		O.C. Companys visited the line. 2/Lt SWAIN returned from leave to the U.K. They were night firing was carried out last night. Weather very fair situation quiet.	Ypres
	27.		O.C. Company visited all guns with the Brigade Major. There was a thick mist all morning. The usual night firing was carried out last night. Weather fair situation very quiet.	Ypres
	28		Enemy Artillery rather more active. The usual night firing was carried out last night. Weather fine	Ypres
	29.		O.C. Company visited the line had night enemy considerably	

Army Form C. 2118.

WAR DIARY
or
INTELLIGENCE SUMMARY.

(Erase heading not required.) Page 19.

Place	Date	Hour	Summary of Events and Information	Remarks and references to Appendices
ST LEGER	29.		Made several bombing raids on enemy area during 10.15 pm. The company Transport lines were at MOYVIC CAMP NOYEN-VIRE were bombed. 5 Bombs were dropped, one being a D.D. 2 Horses were killed and 12 wounded. The usual night firing was carried out.	
	30.		Arranged that the company would be relieved at 7 am M.B. Company on the 31st. Weather fine. O.C. 24th M.G. by friends O.C. Company & arrange details of relief. O.C. Company visited Transport lines weather us.	these
	31st		24th M.G. Coy relieves the Company and not return conduct by 6 pm. after why the Company Relay was to BURTOW CAMP. was carried out last night weather wet	these

A(092). Wt. W12839/M7097 750,000. 1/17. D.B & L. Ltd. Forms/C2118/4.

WAR DIARY
or
INTELLIGENCE SUMMARY

Appendix I

Strength of Company - January 1st   10 Off 179 O.R.
              "   "   31st   11 Off 165 O.R.

              "   "   Attacks.

Increase 1 Officer
Decrease 14 O.R.

Casualties Nil.

Courses   4 O.R.   Bombing School.
          1 O.R.   P.T.B.T.
          4 O.R.   Signalling   "
          1 O.R.   Transport   "

S.A.A. Expended 47000 r.v.

Army Form C. 2118.

WAR DIARY
or
INTELLIGENCE SUMMARY.

(Erase heading not required.)

WAR DIARY

119 Machine Gun Company

February 1916

Copy I

Army Form C. 2118.

WAR DIARY
or
INTELLIGENCE SUMMARY.

Page 1

(Erase heading not required.)

Instructions regarding War Diaries and Intelligence Summaries are contained in F.S. Regs., Part II. and the Staff Manual respectively. Title pages will be prepared in manuscript.

Place	Date	Hour	Summary of Events and Information	Remarks and references to Appendices
ERVILLERS	1.		The Company was out of the line and carried out training and wiring of huts. Weather very cold, situation quiet.	MAP
	2.		The Company training & wiring continued. Three men who had not been inoculated were done by the 137th Field Ambulance. A training area and circus was built by enemy aircraft during the night.	MAP
	3.		Company had usual training the morning. Recreational training & a cinema show in the afternoon. Weather still fine but cold.	MAP
	4.		Company training was carried out. M, 2/Lt E. Kempsall came and found the company from the base after states leave.	MAP
	5.		No 1 Section relieved No 2 Section in the line at ECOUST. 0103 and 2/Lt H. Belcher went up to take a written handover from the	MAP

Army Form C. 2118.

WAR DIARY
or
INTELLIGENCE SUMMARY.
(Erase heading not required.)

Sheet 2

Place	Date	Hour	Summary of Events and Information	Remarks and references to Appendices
ERVILLERS	5.		Ration parties for M.G's. were elected and certain alterations made to the M.G. Scheme of the two right Platoons. Weather mild.	AAP
	6.		The usual duties services were held. O.C. Company visited the HQ. and O.C. 144 M.C. Coy to arrange the relief tomorrow. No. 29053 Sgt MacQuean was awarded the D.C.M. on the New Year Honours List.	—
	7.		The company relieved 244 Machine Gun Company in the left Sector. Relief was complete by 3.30 pm. At 4.30 pm. the S.O.S. was sent up from the right Company and entire Brigade front company opened fire immediately. All our guns continued firing for three quarters of an hour. 10,000 rounds were fired. The rest of the night was quiet. O.C. Company left to join No 46 Squadron R.F.C. for a three days course in Anti-Aircraft	AAP

Army Form C. 2118.

WAR DIARY
or
INTELLIGENCE SUMMARY.
(Erase heading not required.)

Page II

Instructions regarding War Diaries and Intelligence Summaries are contained in F.S. Regs., Part II. and the Staff Manual respectively. Title pages will be prepared in manuscript.

Place	Date	Hour	Summary of Events and Information	Remarks and references to Appendices
ERMINERS	5		Intermediate area near ECOUST. Weather fine	
	6		Weather wet. Capt R.T Carnoncross M.C. proceeded on leave to the U.K.	
			At 7.E. At 7.E. Edwards M.C. returned from leave to the U.K. No 1 Section has entre.	MAP
	7		At Rungin proceeded on recon to the United Kingdom. Company training and rusetting of huts continued. Weather fine	
	8		Weather very wet. Instructor training carried on	MAP
	9		No 3 Section went up to amplifi the Battery trenchwon sys the other night. No 1 Section was inoculated	
	10		Church parade under At Andechem in the morning	
			Recreational training in the afternoon. At P Bunker recommoiged NEUVILLE VITASSE	MAP

Army Form C. 2118.

WAR DIARY
or
INTELLIGENCE SUMMARY.
(Erase heading not required.)

Page 14

Place	Date	Hour	Summary of Events and Information	Remarks and references to Appendices
ERVILLERS	11		Return officers proceeded in advance of the Company to take over Billets had in. The Company marched from ERVILLERS to NEUVILLE VITASSE where they were guided into Billets. Headquarters and No 2 Platoon accommodated at the SUGAR FACTORY NEUVILLE VITASSE. Relief complete with Lt? [unclear]	McP
NEUVILLE-VITASSE	12		at 1.50 p.m. 2/15 Queen returned from leave. O.C. Company + 2/c visited the line weather very wet and foggy.	McP
	13		Rain fell all the morning so that it was impossible to do any training with the Reserve Platoon. Situation very quiet.	McP

Army Form C. 2118.

WAR DIARY
or
INTELLIGENCE SUMMARY.

Page IV

(Erase heading not required.)

Instructions regarding War Diaries and Intelligence Summaries are contained in F. S. Regs., Part II. and the Staff Manual respectively. Title pages will be prepared in manuscript.

Place	Date	Hour	Summary of Events and Information	Remarks and references to Appendices
NEUVILLE VITASSE.	14.		20 men were taken on the strength of the Company as attached from the Infantry. Situation quiet. Working parties were sent up the line at night. Weather wet.	Map.
	15.		Attacks men and reserve section carried out training. Nothing doing. Parties were again sent up to dig emplacements. Work on the Coy. and emplacements. Situation quiet. Weather fair	
	16.		No 1 Section carried on training. Weather fair.	
	17.		5 O.R. joined the Company from the Base. Training carried on. Situation very quiet. Weather fine.	
	18.		Training carried on. Situation very quiet. Weather fair.	Maps.

Army Form C. 2118.

WAR DIARY
or
INTELLIGENCE SUMMARY.

Page V

(Erase heading not required.)

Place	Date	Hour	Summary of Events and Information	Remarks and references to Appendices
NEUVILLE VITASSE	19.		Reserve sections were put on cleaning limbers and Ramers for an inspection on the 26th. Lively aft the Company to join the 9th Entrenching Battn. Quiet. Weather fair.	MAP
	20.		Transport inspection cancelled. 2/Lt Wickham was absent. Transport officer. Situation quiet. Weather fair.	
	21.		Training continues. No 1 section Parades for work at 3rd Battn HQ. Situation quiet. Weather fair.	MAP
	22.		Capt D.S. Cunningham M.C. returned from leave to the U.K. Lt J.E. Colringer M.C. went sick and was evacuated	MAP

WAR DIARY
or
INTELLIGENCE SUMMARY.

Army Form C. 2118.

Page VI

Place	Date	Hour	Summary of Events and Information	Remarks and references to Appendices
NEUVILLE VITASSE			to the Casualty Clearing Station. Training continues Situation quiet, weather fair.	AWP
	23		O.C. Company & 2/c reconnoitred the line. Training continued. Situation quiet, weather fair.	
	24		O.C. Company attended a conference of Company Commanders and the new Battalion Commander at Brigade. Details for the formation of the Machine Gun Battalion were gone into. Situation Quiet, weather fair.	AWP
	25		The new Machine Gun Battalion was formed at 9 am. today. Orders were received that the Company would by on the 27th instant relieved by the 12th M.G. Coy.	AWP

Army Form C. 2118.

WAR DIARY
or
INTELLIGENCE SUMMARY.

(Erase heading not required.)

Page VIII

Place	Date	Hour	Summary of Events and Information	Remarks and references to Appendices
NEUVE EGLISE	26th		Situation quiet. Weather fine. The name of the Company was changed to "A" Company 40th Divisional M.-G. Battalion. A Field Kitchen allowed by the new Company Establishment was drawn. Recommendations were made from the 120 M.-G. Coy. invited to Capt. Botting. Situation Quiet. Weather fair.	ALS
	27th		The Company was relieved by the 120 M.-G. Company relief being complete at 2.30 pm. after which the Company marched to INNISKILLEN CAMP ERYKKERS. Situation quiet. Weather fair.	ALS

Army Form C. 2118.

WAR DIARY
or
INTELLIGENCE SUMMARY.

(Erase heading not required.)

Page VIII

Place	Date	Hour	Summary of Events and Information	Remarks and references to Appendices
ERVILLERS	28		The Company marches from ERVILLERS to ARMAGH CAMP HAMELINCOURT and arrives at about 11 a.m. A conference of company commanders was held at Bn. H.Q. at ARMAGH CAMP. Orders to the financial status of the Battalion written. gone	AAQR

WAR DIARY or **INTELLIGENCE SUMMARY**
Army Form C. 2118.

Appendix 1

Strength of Company Feb 1st   10 Off – 165 O.R.
     "   "   Feb 28th   10 Off – 169 O.R.

Interval.   A.O.R.
Casualties   Nil.
Courses   P.B. & T.
                  M-G. School   1 Sergeant
                  "Transport"   1 cpl
                  M.L.   1 Servant
Rounds fired

www.ingramcontent.com/pod-product-compliance
Lightning Source LLC
Chambersburg PA
CBHW081526160426
43191CB00011B/1693